FOOD FROM MANY GREEK KITCHENS

Andrews McMeel Publishing, LLC
an Andrews McMeel Universal company
1130 Walnut Street, Kansas City, Missouri 64106

www.andrewsmcmeel.com

First published in 2010 by Murdoch Books Pty Ltd
Pier 8/9, 23 Hickson Road, Millers Point NSW 2000

Food from Many Greek Kitchens © 2011 by Murdoch Books Pty Ltd
Text copyright © 2011 by Tessa Kiros
Photographs copyright © 2011 by Manos Chatzikonstantis

11 12 13 14 15 MUB 10 9 8 7 6 5 4 3 2 1

ISBN: 978-1-4494-0652-3

Library of Congress Control Number: 2010943021

Publisher: Kay Scarlett
Photography: Manos Chatzikonstantis
Illustrations and Styling: Michail Touros
Art Direction and Design: Lisa Greenberg
Editor: Daniela Bertollo
Food Editor: Jo Glynn
Designer: Clare O'Loughlin
Production: Joan Beal
Color reproduction by Splitting Image Colour Studio, Melbourne, Australia.

OVEN VARIATION: You may find cooking times vary depending on the oven you are using.
For fan-forced ovens, as a general rule, set the oven temperature to 35°F lower than indicated in
the recipe.

ATTENTION: SCHOOLS AND BUSINESSES
Andrews McMeel books are available at quantity discounts with bulk purchase for educational,
business, or sales promotional use. For information, please e-mail the Andrews McMeel
Publishing Special Sales Department: specialsales@amuniversal.com

FOOD FROM MANY GREEK KITCHENS

Tessa Kiros

**Andrews McMeel
Publishing, LLC**
Kansas City • Sydney • London

FOR GREECE:
*May your ancient
Gods and Goddesses watch
over you always*

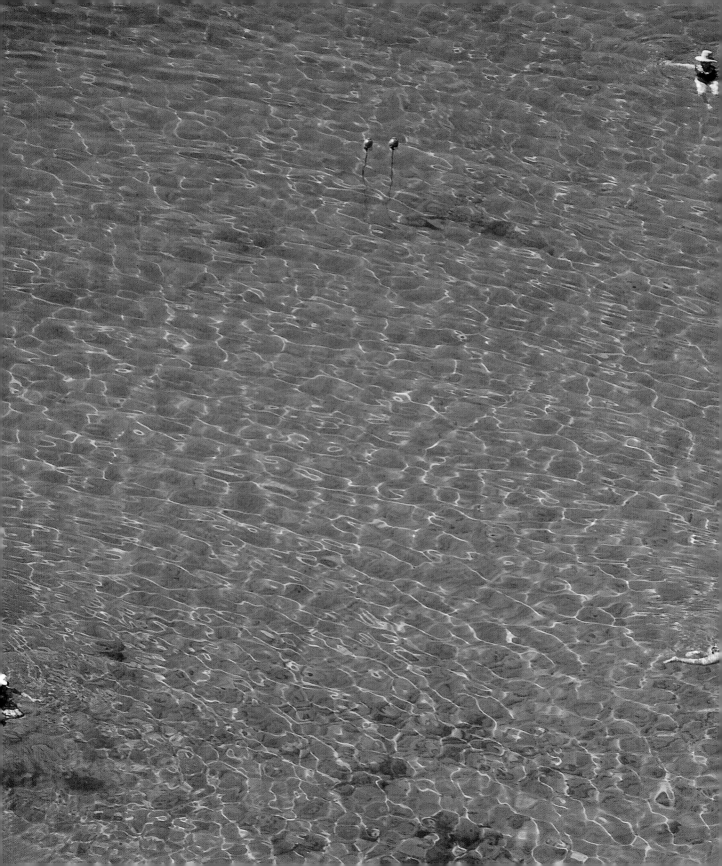

INTRODUCTION

A α

(alfa) is for Artemis, goddess of the hunt and of the moon. And Athena, the goddess of Athens, who gave her name to the capital of Greece. For Achilleas–the "invincible" Trojan War hero with the vulnerable heel. Anithos (dill)–much used in greek dishes. Arni–lamb. And agapi–love.

B b

(vita) like vassilopitta–the cake with the coin that brings in the New Year. Also for vasilias–king, and vasilissa–queen.

Γ γ

(yamma) like yiaourti (yogurt) that in Greece needs no introduction. Partnered with savory foods, or as a dessert with honey and nuts can't be bettered. Also for yelio–laughter.

Δ δ

(delta) for Dionyssos–the god of wine and ylenti (good times, party). Or diosmos–mint, a nice surprise here and there in Greek cooking. And daphne–bay leaves–used regularly. Also for Delphi–the place where the most famous ancient oracle was housed.

E ε

(epsilon) is for elies–olives, ellines–Greeks and their wonderful spirit. Efcharisto–thanks, and Eros–the god of love.

Z ζ

(zita) as in zeimbekiko, the Greek dance that no one can teach you. Dance it when you are blue. It is said that "to learn zeimbekiko, you have to have loved, been hurt, cried and suffered first. Then it comes to you." Also for zoi–life, zòo–animal and zachari–sugar.

Ηη

(ita) as in Hera, the goddess of family and Dias' (Zeus') wife. Also for Helios . . . so much sun and warmth that people are led to Greece for.

Θη

(theta) as in thalassa–the sea and so very very much of it that has shaped Greece's past and present. Also for thimari–thyme.

Ιι

(yiota) Ippocrates–the father of medicine. Ithaki–Odysseus' much longed-for island and final destination.

Κκ

(kappa) Karavi–boat. Or kaiki (caique)–the traditional Greek boat that can safely sway right down on its side and then bounce right back with the waves. Kyrie Eleison (Lord have mercy). Krassi–wine. And for the city of Kalamata with its wonderful olives.

Λλ

(lamda) for lambada, the natural wax candle. Lagana–the bread eaten just before Easter. And for limani (port) and the laiki agora (street market selling fresh produce).

Μμ

(mi) is for Mykonos, and Minos, the ancient king of Crete. Mycenae (one of Greece's ancient kingdoms ruled by King Agamemnon). And Mani on the mainland of the Peloponnese. Also for Mati–the eye intended as the evil eye. Meli–which is honey. And the great actress Melina Mercouri.

Ν ν

(ni) as in Nissi–island. Hundreds of nissia. And nero–water.

Ξ ξ

(xi) Xenos–foreigner/stranger. Xigala, a lovely, soft, slightly sour cheese from Crete–eaten with bread as a starter. Xidi (vinegar) and Xifias (swordfish).

Ο ο

(omikron) as in Olympus, the mount of the gods. And Homer's *Odyssey*. The Olympic games, which started in the ancient city of Olympia. In Greek the "o" and "u" together make a U sound as in ouzo.

Π π

(pi) as in the Parthenon–the temple of Athena on the Acropolis. And for periptero–the many handy small, always open kiosks on the side of roads in Greece that sell everything. For the lovely island of Patmos . . . where it is said that John received the apocalypse or revelation. And for Poseidon–god of the sea.

Ρ ρ

(ro) as in revithia–chickpeas. And raki–the strong Cretan digestive spirit.

Σ σ

(sigma) as in Smyrni in Asia Minor (now Izmir in Turkey). It was inhabited by thousands of Greeks who were then evicted by the Turks in 1922. Some influences remain in dishes such as soutzoukakia (meatballs in tomato with cumin).

Ττ

(taf) is for tiropita–cheese pie. Trapezi–table, and tavli–backgammon (a national pastime in Greece). And for taverna–a traditional Greek restaurant.

Υυ

(ipsilon) as in Hydra, the beautiful car-free island. Hypervoli (exaggeration). Hyperifanos (proud). And for Hygia (health).

Φφ

(fi) as in filia (friendship). Fotia (fire). Feggari (the moon). Fistikia–pistachio nuts–that the island of Aegina is so well known for.

Χχ

(xi) the island of Xios (Chios) and its wonderful masticha–a resin from the masticha trees used as an ingredient in some traditional ice creams, and in some breads like tsoureki.

Ψψ

(psi) as in psomi–bread, or psomaki–small breads (the much-used diminutive in the Greek language). Psari–fish from the abundant waters, and psaras–fisherman. Psachno–to search, and psychi–soul.

Ωω

(omega) as in "the alpha and omega of it all."

Mükovo

KOREAN AIR

see CUBA

DNEY

Singapore

gin express

TRAVEL

GREECE - ITALY
SUPERFAST

RHODES

Rhodes   Naxos

SKIATHOS   PAROS   SKIATHOS

g
U

Gre
the u
choic

Meet the new Gre

ONE DAY CRUISE
POROS - HYDRA - AEGINA

CYCLADES

SKIATHOS

ANCONA LINE

DOMESTIC ROUTES

CONTENTS

GLOSSARY

A

ALATOPIPERIGANO
seasoning made from
salt, black pepper and
dried oregano.

ANTHONERO
flower petal water.

ANTHOTIRO
a soft, white, creamy cheese,
similar to ricotta.

AVGOLEMONO
made from lemon juice and
beaten egg, widely used to
thicken soups and for sauces.

B

BAKALIAROS
salt cod that needs to be
soaked in fresh water for
several days to soften the
flesh and remove the salt.

BRIKI
long-handled coffee pot,
which comes in different sizes
and is made from various
metals such as copper,
stainless steel and aluminum.

C

CAPER LEAVES
pickled caper sprigs with
leaves are available in jars
from Greek grocery stores.

CELERY
Greek celery is thinner and
smaller than regular celery
and is stronger in flavor.
It has lovely green ribs
and leaves—both are used
in cooking.

CHORTA
also spelled horta, wild leafy
greens found everywhere
in Greece.

F

FAVA
name of the dish usually
made with dried split yellow
peas and sometimes yellow
lentils or dried yellow fava
beans.

FETA CHEESE
most commonly made now
using cow's milk, but also
still made with sheep's or
goat's milk.

FLORINIS
small sweet red bell peppers
from the Florina region in
Greece. Lovely roasted.

FRIGANIES
dried bread cut into
thin slices.

G

GLISTRIDA
Greek for purslane. Used
fresh in salads or cooked
as you would spinach. Also
known as andrakla.

GRATING OR SHREDDING
Grating onions and tomatoes
gives a fine, soft texture
without puréeing them.

GREEK YOGURT
thicker and creamier
than regular yogurts.

H

HILOPITES
rough-cut squares of noodles/
pasta, often homemade but
can be bought dried.

HORIATIKI
also spelled choriatiki, the
traditional Greek salad.

K

KAIMAKI
ice cream often flavored
with masticha and sometimes
with salepi.

KALAMAKI
literally, "little reed."
These are the wooden
skewers and also refer to
the souvlaki proper.

KASSERI
medium-hard sheep's milk
cheese similar to pecorino.

KRITHARAKI
orzo or rice-shaped
dried pasta.

L

LADOLEMONO
a sauce or dressing made
with lemon juice and oil.

M

MASTICHA
also spelled mastic, tree resin
used for flavoring as well as
for its gum properties.

MEZE
small dishes or appetizers
to be shared.

MIZITHRA
an almost sweet, hard white
cheese often grated over
cooked dishes. Can also be
soft like ricotta.

O

OKRA
also known as lady's
fingers, this mucilaginous
plant is greatly appreciated
in cooking.

OREGANO
used dried in Greek
cooking. If possible,
buy bunches imported
from Greece (wrapped
in cellophane) from
Greek grocery stores.

OUZO
the popular, licorice-flavored
apéritif that magically
changes color when water or
ice is added.

P

PHYLLO PASTRY
also spelled filo. Different
manufacturers make sheets
of different dimensions
and thicknesses.

R

RAKI
also called tsikoudia, it is
a clear spirit.

RICE
a medium-grain rice,
called Karolina, is most
often used in Greece for
stuffing or dolmades.

S

SAGANAKI
little single-serve skillets.
The most popular saganaki is
made with slices of a cheese
such as kefalotiri, kasseri or
sheep's milk feta.

SALEPI
also spelled sahlepi,
a flavoring made from
the ground roots of wild
orchids.

SIKOTARIA
lamb intestines used in the
traditional Easter soup.

T

TAPSI
a baking dish, usually metal,
with low sides. Most Greek
housewives have a number of
different sizes and shapes.

TARAMA
also spelled taramas, it's
salted and cured caviar of
cod, gray mullet or carp.

TRAHANA
also spelled trachanas,
cracked wheat mixed with
yogurt and then dried.

TRADITIONAL

FOODS

Tradition goes that vassilopitta is what you will eat in the New Year. Everyone has a vassilopitta at New Years. Even in many schools, each class gets one. And the truly wonderful thing about this cake is that a flouri (coin) is dropped in before baking. The idea is that no one knows where the coin is. Before serving, slices are cut and named—one for the Virgin Mary, one for Christ, one for the poor, one for the household, and then from the oldest member of the family or friends present, each gets a piece. The nominated pieces are then distributed, and if you are the lucky one to have the coin hidden in your piece of cake, you will be blessed for the whole year. Don't you love that sense of celebration and tradition the Greeks have?

VASSILOPITTA NEW YEAR WISH CAKE

Βασιλόπιτα

MAKES 1 BIG CAKE

1 COIN, SUCH AS A QUARTER OR A DIME

3 CUPS ALL-PURPOSE FLOUR

3 HEAPING TEASPOONS BAKING POWDER

PINCH OF SALT

14 TABLESPOONS (1¾ STICKS) BUTTER, ROOM TEMPERATURE

1½ CUPS SUGAR

4 EGGS

1 TEASPOON VANILLA EXTRACT

1 TABLESPOON GRATED ORANGE ZEST

1 TABLESPOON GRATED LEMON ZEST

¼ CUP BRANDY

¾ CUP MILK

⅓ CUP BLANCHED ALMONDS, FINELY CHOPPED

CONFECTIONERS' SUGAR, FOR DUSTING

You may find different versions of the vassilopitta, from a regular cake like this one to a yeasted bread with different spices. If you don't bake the cake with the flouri (coin) in, once it's baked you can turn the cake over and push a sharp knife into a selected spot, making a thin slit about 1¼ inches deep. Insert the flouri into the slit, then turn the cake back to the right way up so nobody can tell where the coin is.

Preheat the oven to 350°F. Butter and flour a 11¼-inch springform cake pan. Rinse the coin, dry it well and wrap it tightly in aluminum foil. Sift the flour, baking powder and a pinch of salt together into a bowl.

Whip the butter and sugar together with handheld beaters in a large bowl until creamy.

Add the eggs one at a time, whisking each one in well. Beat in the vanilla and the orange and lemon zests. Fold in the dry ingredients alternately with the brandy and the milk, then fold in the almonds. Scrape into the pan. Drop in the coin now, trying to keep it upright, not flat. Bake for 50 to 60 minutes or until a skewer inserted into the center comes out clean. Cool in the pan for 5 minutes before turning out onto a wire cake rack to cool completely.

Put a doily on top of the cake and dust with confectioners' sugar before removing it to reveal a lacy pattern. You can also cut a stencil of the numbers of the new year you are in (e.g., 2011) and dust that. Cut a piece for everybody and serve.

YAMOPILAFO WEDDING RICE

Γαμοπίλαφο

SERVES 4 OR SO

1 SMALL SHOULDER OF
LAMB (ABOUT 1 POUND
5 OUNCES), CUT INTO
2–3 PIECES, THROUGH THE
BONE, BY YOUR BUTCHER

3 TABLESPOONS OLIVE OIL

2 WHITE ONIONS, FINELY
CHOPPED

1 BAY LEAF

2 GARLIC CLOVES, FINELY
CHOPPED

1 TEASPOON GROUND
CINNAMON

SALT AND FRESHLY GROUND
BLACK PEPPER

½ CUP WHITE WINE

1¼ CUPS MEDIUM-GRAIN
RICE

1½ TABLESPOONS BUTTER

COARSELY SHREDDED
ANTHOTIRO, FIRM MIZITHRA
OR SALTED RICOTTA
CHEESE, FOR SERVING

SMALL HANDFUL COARSELY
CHOPPED ITALIAN PARSLEY,
FOR SERVING

Most probably you will have more than four guests for this occasion (which is what this recipe serves), but it is easy to increase these amounts.

The lamb can be served separately as a second course if you like. Also, you can add a chicken for depth in flavor as they do in Crete, which is where this dish is from.

Traditionally staka (a butter made from goat's milk) is added. All this richness should cut through the raki and various wines drunk at the wedding celebration. The next morning (a taxi driver told me), after dancing all night, a mug of rooster broth is had by all the party animals, along with a plate of hilopites (noodles) with coarsely shredded mizithra over the top. This should settle the stomach and give one new energy for the day just dawned.

Rinse the lamb and wipe it all over with a damp cloth. Pat dry. Heat the oil in a heavy-bottomed pot that has a lid and fry the skin side of the lamb pieces until golden brown. Turn them over and when the new underside is starting to brown, add the onion and bay leaf around the sides. Fry them, stirring, until golden, along with the lamb. Add the garlic to the onion and sprinkle the cinnamon and some salt and pepper over the lamb. Stir through and cook until the garlic starts to smell good, then stir in the wine. When most of it has evaporated, add 2 cups of hot water. Bring to a boil, cover with a lid and simmer for 1 hour. Add another cup of water, turn the lamb over and simmer for about 30 minutes more, turning once or twice, or until the meat is falling off the bone. Remove the lamb and keep it warm and covered. Stir the rice into the pot and add 4 cups of hot water. Simmer, covered, until most of the liquid has been absorbed, about 20 minutes. Season with salt.

When the rice is almost ready, remove the lamb bones and shred the meat. Add the butter to the rice and turn through. Serve the rice in bowls with some shredded lamb on top, a scattering of cheese and then parsley and a grind of pepper.

OPA!
AN EXCLAMATION USED WHEN SINGING OR DANCING . . .

BAKLAVADAKIA SMALL BAKLAVA

Μπακλαβαδάκια

MAKES 56

SYRUP

1 CUP SUGAR

4½ TABLESPOONS MILD
RUNNY HONEY

ABOUT ¾ CUP (1½ STICKS)
BUTTER

ABOUT 1¼ POUNDS PHYLLO
PASTRY (13 SHEETS OF
19 X 14½ INCHES)

1½ CUPS SHELLED
UNSALTED PISTACHIO NUTS

These are my favorite baklava: individual small ones packed row by row into a large tray. It's quite easy and totally worth it when you get your head around the math. It may even give you a wonderful sense of achievement when they come out of the oven. The oven dish size, 10 × 12 inches with straight sides, is important to give you 8 rows of 7 baklava (56 baklava). If your dish size is different, you may have to adjust the amount of baklava for a packed-in result full of rows and rows of baklava.
Also, the dimensions and weight of commercial phyllo varies from brand to brand, and so you might need some additional math to work out the number of sheets to use.

To make the syrup, stir the sugar and honey with 9½ ounces of water in a saucepan until the sugar dissolves, then bring to a boil. Simmer for about 10 minutes or until slightly thickened. Cool.

Preheat the oven to 350°F. Melt the butter in a small saucepan until pale golden and smelling great. Cover the phyllo sheets with a clean dry dish cloth to stop them from drying out while you work. Spread one sheet of phyllo on your work surface. Brush gently but well and generously all over with butter. Cover with the next sheet of phyllo, brush with butter and continue in this way until you have a stack of 6 sheets. Using a ruler and a sharp knife, measure and cut 2¾-inch squares. Fill and form this batch before buttering the next so that the phyllo won't dry.

Working quickly, drop about 4 pistachios into the center of each square. Bring the four sides together to form a boat, then pinch them together at about two-thirds of the way up so the points of the phyllo open out like petals. Don't press the top leaves together, as their layerings are important for look and taste. Make sure that the bases are kept as square as possible, and they should measure about 1¼ inches square.

Brush the base and sides of a 10½ × 12-inch baking dish with melted butter. Line up the baklava in neat compact rows like bonbons in a chocolate box. Repeat the full procedure with another 6 sheets of phyllo and continue until you have made 56 baklava. If you are respecting the measures given here, you may need to fold and cut a single phyllo sheet to make up the last few. Flick a little cold water over them with your fingers. Bake for 25 to 30 minutes, until crisp and pale golden.

Drizzle half the syrup evenly over the hot baklava in long thin drizzles. Chop the remaining pistachios finely and scatter some over each baklava. Drizzle over the rest of the syrup to hold the nuts in place. Cool before serving. Keep, unrefrigerated, in the dish in which it's made, covered or in a leakproof cake box of the type that you'd get from a store.

BAKLAVA

Μπακλαβάς

MAKES ABOUT 30

SYRUP

2 CUPS SUGAR

2 TABLESPOONS HONEY

JUICE OF ½ LEMON

STRIP OF LEMON PEEL

2 OR 3 SMALL CINNAMON STICKS

1 CUP ALMONDS, CRUSHED BUT WITH SOME TEXTURE

1 CUP WALNUTS, CRUSHED BUT WITH SOME TEXTURE

2 TABLESPOONS SUGAR

2 TEASPOONS GROUND CINNAMON

22 SHEETS PHYLLO PASTRY*, CUT TO THE DIMENSIONS OF YOUR DISH

ABOUT ⅔ CUP (1¼ STICKS) UNSALTED BUTTER, MELTED TO GOLDEN BROWN

30 OR SO WHOLE CLOVES, FOR DECORATING

I love this Chanel bag–looking thing. It is served, most often with a glass of water, throughout the year and at most celebrations, and on Sundays too. Working with phyllo may take a little getting used to. You need to work quickly so that the pastry doesn't dry out and gently so that it doesn't tear. You may find it easier (at least for the first 10 layers) to put a layer onto your work surface, brush with butter, then put another layer of phyllo neatly over that, smoothing it down as you would the sheets of a bed that you were making. Repeat until all your layers are on, then the pile of sheets can be lowered into your dish.

Preheat the oven to 350°F. To make the syrup, put the sugar, honey, lemon juice, lemon peel and cinnamon in a saucepan with 1 cup water and bring to a boil, stirring. Simmer for 5 to 6 minutes, then take off the heat and cool.

Mix the almonds, walnuts, sugar and cinnamon together in a bowl. Have the phyllo sheets ready, covered by a dish cloth to prevent them from drying out. Brush the base of an 8½ × 12-inch baking dish with butter. Lay 1 sheet of phyllo on the bottom and brush with butter. Cover with another sheet, brush it with butter and continue in this way until you have a neat stack of 10 sheets lining the bottom of the dish. Spread half the nut mixture over the phyllo, patting it down firmly and leveling the surface. Cover with another 2 sheets of phyllo, buttering each one. Scatter the rest of the nuts over evenly and press down gently. Now lay down the last 10 sheets of phyllo, buttering each one, of course, and finishing with the last layer buttered.

Using a small sharp knife, cut diamonds on the diagonal of about 2½ × 2½ inches. Cut all the way through the layers of phyllo, as this will make it easier to lift out the pieces when serving. Flick just a little cold water over the top to prevent the layers from curling up. Stud the center of each diamond with a clove. Bake for 25 to 30 minutes or until gently golden on top. Gently pour half the syrup all over the baklava. Wait for it to be absorbed, then pour over the rest. Leave to cool totally before serving. Will keep, unrefrigerated, for at least a week, covered with a dish cloth or foil to deter bees and flies.

* *The dimensions of commercial phyllo change from brand to brand, so you will need to work out the number of phyllo sheets you require in the beginning, according to the maker's dimensions.*

DIPLES
FRIED FOLDS

Δίπλες

MAKES MANY, MANY

6 EGGS, SEPARATED

½ TEASPOON BAKING
POWDER

3⅓ CUPS ALL-PURPOSE
FLOUR

1 TEASPOON VANILLA
EXTRACT

1 TABLESPOON OLIVE OIL

LIGHT OLIVE OIL,
FOR FRYING

SYRUP

2 CUPS MILD HONEY

1 HEAPING TABLESPOON
SUGAR

3 TEASPOONS LEMON JUICE

1 TEASPOON GROUND
CINNAMON, FOR DUSTING

¼ TEASPOON GROUND
CLOVES, FOR DUSTING

3 TABLESPOONS WALNUTS,
FINELY CHOPPED

These are rather celebrational, the kind of thing you'd serve on a name day or take to someone's house for a special event.

This is Roulla's recipe. She showed us how to make them at her house, and it felt like we were preparing for a wedding or 20 name days, we made so many. The rolling and shaping in the pan is not so easy; you may need a few tries before you get the hang of it. The honey to use is important—what you use is what you will find on your plate—so not too strong is best. Roulla used a mild wild thyme honey. Some people leave out the walnuts on top; others sprinkle on some sesame seeds.

These will keep for a few days, preferably covered. This makes a huge amount, so if you like you can even try half a batch.

Whisk the egg whites with handheld beaters until creamy and fluffy. Add the yolks and continue beating for 20 to 30 seconds to reduce the egginess. Transfer to a large bowl, add the baking powder and start adding the flour, mixing it first with a wooden spoon then changing to your hands as it gets stiffer. Add flour until you have a soft, non-sticky dough. Add the vanilla and knead it in. Lastly add the olive oil and knead until you have a smooth, soft dough. Mark a cross on the top with the edge of your hand, cover the bowl with a dish cloth and leave at room temperature for 30 minutes or so.

Divide the dough in half. Scatter some flour onto a large work surface. Stretch one piece of dough and start flattening it with your hands. Take over with a rolling pin and roll it as thinly as possible to a rough oval about 27½ × 18 inches. Cut 4½-inch-wide strips, then cut in the opposite direction to give lengths of 3½ inches. Once cut, these can be rolled or stretched with your hands to 6 × 4½ inches. Lay, not touching, on a couple of dish cloths and cover with more dish cloths to prevent them from drying out. Repeat the rolling and cutting with the second half of the dough.

Pour oil into a large nonstick skillet to a depth of ¾ inch and put over medium-high heat. Lay the first dough rectangle in the oil. With a fork in each hand, press down on each end of the dough to prevent it from turning up. Then with one fork grab the middle of the dough from underneath and flip it so it folds once on itself, then roll

it with the fork in the middle as though you were rolling a forkful of spaghetti. Fry until crisp and golden, about 20 seconds, holding it to keep its shape and turning it over if necessary. Using the forks, lift it from the oil and tilt it over the pan for a couple of seconds to drain off excess oil. Place it on a tray lined with paper towels. Fry the rest of the dough strips in this way, stacking them in a large dish once they have drained. Reduce the oil temperature if it becomes too hot at any time.

For the syrup, put the honey in a wide pot and add the sugar and 3½ ounces of water. Bring slowly to a boil and as soon as it reaches boiling point, remove it from the heat. Add the lemon juice. Drop in the diples, one at a time, and leave for 30 seconds or so to drink in the honey. Turn

continued

over, leave a bit longer and then lift out with your forks, tilting it to drain off excess honey. Stack them in a large roasting dish and once you have a full layer, lightly dust the tops with cinnamon. Turn them over and dust the other side, this time with just a hint of cloves as well. Sprinkle the tops lightly with walnuts, then continue dipping, layering and dusting. When you have finished you may feel surprised that you have made these. I would suggest that you make them the day before you want to serve them so that you are not all hot and flustered, with a kitchen that needs cleaning just before people arrive.

Name days are given a lot of importance in Greece—it seems easier for some to remember a name than a date of birth. And then anyway all the Nikos can celebrate together one day, the Marias another and some overlap like St. Constantine and St. Helen on the same day . . . (and so there can be much celebration together).

FANOUROPITA CAKE FOR LOST THINGS

Φανουρόπιτα

MAKES 1 CAKE

3¾ CUPS ALL-PURPOSE FLOUR

1 TABLESPOON BAKING POWDER

¾ CUP PLUS 2 TABLESPOONS SUGAR

1 TEASPOON GROUND CINNAMON

¾ CUP LIGHT OLIVE OIL

¾ CUP FRESH ORANGE JUICE

1 TEASPOON VANILLA EXTRACT

This simple, easy to whip together cake is made in honor of St. Fanourios, the patron saint of lost things. The day before St. Fanourios day, one can imagine the scent of cakes baking filling kitchens everywhere. They are taken to church the following day, where they are blessed and then shared among the people. A fanouropita can be made any time of year, though—when something is lost such as a ring, or a lover or even when a mind is in search of an answer. The cake is ideal during the fasting period, as it has no eggs and no butter.

Preheat the oven to 375°F. Brush a 9½-inch springform cake pan with oil, and flour it. In a bowl stir the flour, baking powder, sugar and cinnamon together. Add the olive oil, orange juice and vanilla and whisk with handheld beaters until combined. It will be very thick. Scrape into your pan and bake until a skewer inserted into the center comes out clean, about 40 minutes. Cool on a wire cake rack before cutting and distributing appropriately. Keeps well for 5 to 6 days in an airtight container.

KOURABIEDES BUTTERY ALMOND CAKES

Κουραμπιέδες

MAKES ABOUT 22

⅓ CUP ALMONDS, SKIN ON

1 CUP PLUS 2 TABLESPOONS (2¼ STICKS) BUTTER, ROOM TEMPERATURE

2 TABLESPOONS CONFECTIONERS' SUGAR

1 EGG YOLK

1 TEASPOON VANILLA EXTRACT

1 TABLESPOON BRANDY

2 CUPS ALL-PURPOSE FLOUR

1 TEASPOON BAKING POWDER

2 CUPS CONFECTIONERS' SUGAR, FOR DUSTING

These are sugary, buttery, melt-in-your-mouth honest bundles enjoyed at Christmas.

Chop the almonds into small pieces. Toast in a dry skillet over low-ish heat until just colored, then cool.

Whisk the butter in a bowl using handheld beaters until very pale and thick, about 8 minutes. Add the confectioners' sugar and whisk it in well. Add the egg yolk, vanilla and brandy and whisk them in well. Sift in the flour and baking powder and beat until you have a smooth dough that is hard to keep mixing with the beaters. Add the almonds and mix in with your hands. Press the dough into a ball, cover with plastic wrap and refrigerate for 30 to 40 minutes.

Meanwhile, preheat the oven to 350°F and line a baking sheet with parchment paper. Break off pieces of dough, about 1¼ ounces each, and roll them into balls, slightly flattening the tops. Put them on the sheet, allowing a little space between each one. Bake until lightly golden, 20 to 25 minutes. Remove from the oven and let cool on the sheet for about 15 minutes.

Dust about half of the confectioners' sugar onto a tray or large plate or your container where you will store them. Gently move the kourabiedes to sit in a single layer in this, then sprinkle the remaining confectioners' sugar over their tops so that they look like they are snowed in. Will keep for many days in a covered container.

MELOMAKARONA HONEY CAKES

Μελομακάρονα

MAKES 15

6 TABLESPOONS SUGAR

¾ CUP EXTRA VIRGIN OLIVE OIL

3 TABLESPOONS BRANDY

JUICE OF ½ ORANGE

1 TEASPOON GRATED ORANGE ZEST

1 TEASPOON BAKING POWDER

½ TEASPOON BAKING SODA

2 TEASPOONS GROUND CINNAMON

¼ TEASPOON GROUND CLOVES

¼ TEASPOON GRATED NUTMEG

2 CUPS ALL-PURPOSE FLOUR

SYRUP

½ CUP HONEY

¾ CUP SUGAR

1 STRIP ORANGE ZEST

1 SMALL CINNAMON STICK

15 WHOLE CLOVES

3 TABLESPOONS CRUSHED WALNUTS, FOR SERVING

This is Katerina's wonderful recipe. Katerina is Trini's cousin. Trini is our photographer Manos' girlfriend. Melomakarona are small cakes drenched in honey syrup, which shout "Christmas" in Greece. Take them as gifts in a box, or eat them slowly throughout the season. You can make them smaller if you like, even half this size (which are truly lovely).

Preheat the oven to 350°F and line a baking sheet with parchment paper. Stir the sugar and oil in a wide bowl until dissolved. Add the brandy, orange juice and zest. Mix the baking powder, baking soda, ground cinnamon, ground cloves and nutmeg into the flour. Add to the bowl and mix to a loose dough with a wooden spoon. Using your hands, knead to a soft and smooth dough.

Break off small clumps of dough of about 1½ ounces each (you should get 15). Roll each into a ball between your palms, then form small ovals of about 2½ × 1½ inches. Set them onto the baking sheet and bake until firm and the bases are gold, about 30 minutes.

While they are baking, make the syrup. Put all the ingredients along with ¾ cup of water in a small pot and stir over medium heat until the sugar dissolves. Simmer for 5 minutes, then keep warm.

Put the cakes in a dish with sides where they will fit in one layer. Stud each with a clove. Pour the syrup over them, covering each well. Leave for 5 minutes. Spoon some syrup (it will be a little thicker now) from the bottom of the dish over the tops of the cakes and sprinkle with the walnuts. Remove to a serving plate. Drizzle the walnuts with remaining syrup. Cover and cool completely. Will keep for many days, stored in a covered container.

TSIKNOPEMPTI

"Tsikna" is the smell of grilled meat and "Pempti" is Thursday. So on this Thursday during carnival, about 1½ weeks before Clean Monday, you will find everyone eating grilled meat. Many people go out to eat in restaurants and to celebrate carnival out in the streets.

PAIDAKIA GRILLED LAMB CUTLETS

Παϊδάκια

SERVES 3 OR 4

2¼ POUNDS LAMB CUTLETS, UNTRIMMED

¼ CUP OLIVE OIL

JUICE OF 2 LEMONS

1 TEASPOON DRIED OREGANO

1 LARGE GARLIC CLOVE, PEELED AND CRUSHED

½ TEASPOON SALT

FRESHLY GROUND BLACK PEPPER

ALATOPIPERIGANO (PAGE 128), FOR SERVING

LEMON WEDGES, FOR SERVING

I love the way you can order these by the pound in some grill places. On the table we always have a dish of tzatziki (page 130), fava (page 74) and a Greek salad (page 223). I also love tirokafteri (spicy feta, page 142) here. You should put some bread slices on the outdoor grill too, just after the meat, grill a bit, then remove to a plate and drizzle the slices with olive oil and scatter with the salt, pepper and crumbled oregano mix (alatopiperigano).

The lamb cutlets are best small with their fat left on, which is great grilled, but of course whoever doesn't like the fat can cut it away.

Rinse the cutlets if necessary, or wipe with damp paper towels and put in a dish. Make the marinade in a bowl with the olive oil, lemon juice, oregano, garlic, salt and a few grinds of pepper. Splash about 4 tablespoons for now over the cutlets, cover with plastic wrap and leave for an hour or so.

Preheat a grill to hot. Put the cutlets on a grill rack about 4 inches from the coals and grill till deep brown and crusty looking here and there on both sides, but not dried out, basting often with the rest of the marinade. Remove to a platter, crumble a little of the alatopiperigano over and serve at once with the lemon wedges.

KATHARI DEFTERA – CLEAN MONDAY

Many people fly a kite on this day and most eat these: taramosalata, dolmades with no meat in the filling, lagana, taramokeftedes and halva. No meat is eaten. Picnics are taken out with these dishes and also vegetables, oysters and other seafood.

LAGANA ONCE-A-YEAR BREAD

Λαγάνα

MAKES 1 BREAD

½ OUNCE FRESH YEAST, OR 2 TEASPOONS ACTIVE DRY YEAST

PINCH OF SUGAR

2⅔ CUPS BREAD FLOUR

½ TEASPOON SALT

¼ CUP OLIVE OIL

TOPPING

1 TABLESPOON BREAD FLOUR

½ TABLESPOON OLIVE OIL

¼ TEASPOON SALT

1½ TABLESPOONS SESAME SEEDS

This is just a once-a-year bread in Greece, for the kite flying and taramokeftedes time. But of course you can make it as many times in the year as you like.

I got this recipe from an old baker in Mesolonghi, who described it as a flat bread with a puckered look on top. And the trick, he says, is the fluid flour and water mixture that gets brushed on before baking. And a good scattering of sesame seeds. Lagana is best eaten on the day made. If you want to make it in advance, seal in a plastic bag and store in the freezer. You can double this recipe and make two loaves, as it's always good to have on a day like Clean Monday. This bread makes great toasts (friganies), cut up the next day and toasted in the oven.

Crumble the fresh yeast or sprinkle the dried yeast into a large bowl. Add the sugar and 7 ounces of lukewarm water and leave until it starts to activate and bubble. Add the flour, salt and olive oil and mix together with a wooden spoon until a loose dough forms. If it seems too dry, then add a few more drops of water. Knead for 6 or 7 minutes on a lightly floured surface, until the dough is smooth and spongy. Wipe out the bowl with oiled paper towels and put the dough in. Cover the bowl with plastic wrap, then a dish cloth, and leave in a warm spot for about 2½ hours, or until puffed and doubled in size. Line a baking sheet with parchment paper. Punch the dough down and shape by stretching and rolling it into a rough rectangle of about 9½ × 12¾ inches and about ⅜ inch thick. Put onto the lined sheet and dent many holes all over the surface with the tips of your fingers for a puckered look. Cover with dish cloths and leave in the warm spot for 30 minutes or so to rise again.

Preheat the oven to 400°F. For the topping, whisk the flour, oil, salt and 2 tablespoons of water together. Gently brush all over the top of the bread, then sprinkle with the sesame seeds. Bake for about 20 minutes or until golden.

TARAMOSALATA

Ταραμοσαλάτα

MAKES JUST OVER 2 CUPS

2 OR 3 BIG SLICES OF
COUNTRY-STYLE BREAD
(ABOUT 3½ OUNCES),
WITHOUT CRUST

4½ OUNCES TARAMA

PINCH OF PAPRIKA

½ RED ONION, PEELED AND
GRATED ON THE LARGE
HOLES OF A GRATER

SCANT 1¼ CUPS LIGHT
OLIVE OIL

JUICE OF 2–2½ LEMONS

This is most often served as a meze, a dip that would precede other dishes, or it stands beautifully among other seafood bits and pieces.

Tarama is salted cod or gray mullet caviar and is a dusty rusty color to start with. Mixed with the other ingredients, its color dilutes to an antique beige-pink. Some people do drop in some food coloring to make it more pink, which is how you might find it here and there. And some use potato instead of bread. Tarama is available in Greek supermarkets and specialty food shops. Taramosalata is wonderful with breads such as lagana (page 50) or koulouria (page 161) and a dish of olives. At first it may taste a little strong, but give it a few hours in the fridge to mellow. The next day it is lovely. Taramosalata will keep well in the fridge, covered, for 2 to 3 days.

Tear up the bread into a bowl. Splash with a little water, just enough to dampen, and leave for a few minutes. Squeeze out all the water and put the bread back in the bowl. Add the tarama, paprika and the onion with its juice.

Whisk with handheld beaters, adding a little of the oil as though you were making mayonnaise. Add a few drops of the lemon juice, beat in, then some oil and continue in this way until all the oil is in and you have enough lemon juice for your taste. Transfer the mixture to a blender and pulse it to give a smooth consistency. If it seems too thick, pulse in a little water.

ΚΑΦΕΠΑΝΤΟΠΩΛΕΙΟΝ
ΤΑ ΨΑΡΑΔΙΚΑ
ΠΛΕΚΤΑ
ΕΣΩΡΟΥΧΑ
Ἀφοί Μέλλιου
MINEPBA
Renee
BERKSHIRE
VIP'S
Le chien
Ἀφοί Μέλλιου
Μ.ΑΛΕΞΑΝΡΟΥ 5
ΦΛΩΡΙΝΑ
22403
ΛΙΝΑΣ Γ. ΧΑΣΟΥ

TARAMOKEFTEDES TARAMA BALLS

Ταραμοκεφτέδες

MAKES ABOUT 24

7 OUNCES CRUSTLESS
DAY-OLD BREAD

1 LARGE GARLIC CLOVE,
PEELED

SALT

2½ OUNCES TARAMA

½ RED ONION, GRATED
ON THE LARGE HOLES
OF A GRATER

1 TEASPOON COARSELY
CHOPPED MINT

1 TABLESPOON COARSELY
CHOPPED ITALIAN PARSLEY

1 TABLESPOON LEMON
JUICE

FRESHLY GROUND BLACK
PEPPER

ALL-PURPOSE FLOUR,
FOR DUSTING

LIGHT OLIVE OIL,
FOR FRYING

1 LEMON, QUARTERED

For these fried tarama balls, you should use a good dense country bread, not the light airy type. These are best eaten on Clean Monday out on a picnic somewhere in the hills. If you want, make them in between flying kites.

This is a lovely meze with ouzo that can mingle well with many dishes —and great, of course, to precede any fish or seafood dish.

Tear the bread into pieces, put in a bowl and splash with just enough water to dampen. Leave for a few minutes, then squeeze it out over the sink until dry. Return the bread to the bowl. Crush the garlic with a pinch of salt into a paste using the flat of your knife, then add to the bread. Add the tarama, onion and its juice, mint, parsley and lemon juice, and a little pepper. Mix thoroughly with your hands. It shouldn't need salt, but taste to see. Shape into balls the size of a small cherry tomato (about ¾ ounce). Leave to rest for 15 minutes or so.

Put some flour on a plate and roll the balls in it to cover them. Add the olive oil to a depth of about ¼ inch in a large nonstick skillet and put over medium-high heat. Add the balls, in batches if necessary, and fry until nicely golden all over, shaking the skillet once or twice to make sure nothing is stuck. Remove with a slotted spoon and drain on a plate lined with paper towels. Sprinkle with a little salt. Eat warm, with a few drops of lemon juice.

DOLMADES STOVETOP STUFFED VINE LEAVES

Ντολμάδες στην κατσαρόλα

MAKES 35 TO 40

35–40 GOOD VINE LEAVES, PLUS A FEW TORN ONES

6 TABLESPOONS OLIVE OIL

2 RED ONIONS, GRATED ON THE LARGE HOLES OF A GRATER

1 CUP MEDIUM-GRAIN RICE

3 LARGE TOMATOES, GRATED ON THE LARGE HOLES OF A GRATER (SO SKINS STAY BEHIND IN YOUR HAND), PLUS 1 EXTRA FOR THE TOPPING

½ CUP CHOPPED ITALIAN PARSLEY

JUICE OF 1 LEMON

1 TEASPOON DRIED MINT

SALT AND FRESHLY GROUND BLACK PEPPER

Bottled and prepacked vine leaves are already blanched and are available from large supermarkets and Greek and Middle Eastern food stores.

To use fresh vine leaves, collect them from the last 8 inches or so of unsprayed young vines. Choose leaves that are roughly the size of your hand and are tender, unmarked and not torn. Cut them off, leaving just ¼ inch of the stem at the base of the leaf. Rinse and drain them twice. Put in stacks of 20 or so, then roll them up into a loose cigar and tie with string. Dip each roll into a pot of boiling water, just in and out, then drain and cool. If you are not going to use them right away, put the rolls in an airtight container and freeze.

This is a lovely, traditional, no-meat version of dolmades, suitable for the fasting period before Easter. These are great with tzatziki (page 130) and are good served warm or at room temperature. Some even love them cold.

Before wrapping up the filling in the leaves, I like to weigh the filling and divide it by the number of leaves. Less precise, but still a good idea, is to divide the mixture into quarters so it's easier to visualize how you are doing amount-wise.

If using bought leaves, put them in a large bowl of cold water to soak for a few minutes. Drain, pat dry with paper towels, then stack in piles for later. Heat 5 tablespoons of the oil in a large skillet with a lid and sauté the onions over medium heat until golden. Add the rice, stir until coated, then add the grated tomato, parsley, lemon juice and mint, and season well with salt and pepper. Put the lid on and simmer for about 10 minutes or until the rice has softened and plumped up and most of the liquid has been absorbed. Remove from the heat and leave with the lid on for 5 minutes or so.

Use a few torn vine leaves to cover the bottom of a wide heavy-bottomed pot. Lay a few whole vine leaves at a time on your work surface, shiny side down. Spoon a heaped tablespoon of filling, about ¾ ounce, onto each leaf and roll it up neatly and quite snugly, tucking in the sides after the first roll and continuing to roll them. Put them in the pot in concentric circles, starting on the outside, and make a second layer if necessary. Grate (so that the skin stays behind in your hand) the remaining tomato over the top, pour in about 3 cups of hot water or enough to cover and drizzle in the remaining oil. Season with a little salt. Put a snug-fitting upturned plate over the top to keep the dolmades submerged. Cover and bring to a boil. Lower the heat and simmer for about 1 hour, until the dolmades are tender and much of the liquid has been absorbed. Turn off the heat and let them rest for 10 minutes or so before serving.

DOLMADES BAKED STUFFED VINE LEAVES

Ντολμάδες στον φούρνο

MAKES 35 TO 40

35–40 GOOD VINE LEAVES, PLUS A FEW TORN ONES

1 RED ONION, PEELED

9 OUNCES WILD OR CREMINI MUSHROOMS

1 CARROT, PEELED

7 OUNCES ZUCCHINI

3 LARGE TOMATOES

ABOUT ¼ CUP OLIVE OIL

½ CUP MEDIUM-GRAIN RICE

3 TABLESPOONS CHOPPED ITALIAN PARSLEY

½ TABLESPOON DRIED MINT

JUICE OF 1 LEMON

SALT AND FRESHLY GROUND BLACK PEPPER

3 TABLESPOONS SHREDDED KEFALOTIRI CHEESE OR PARMESAN

This wonderful recipe comes from my friend Artemis's mother, Christina. It is a more unusual vegetarian version than you may find readily available in Greece and completely delicious.

It is very easy to double the quantity, and they keep well for the next day, so it's worth making a good amount. Christina makes at least 70 at a time—it can be fun to sit at a table and work, maybe with someone helping you.

If using bought leaves, put them in a bowl of water to soak for a few minutes. Drain, pat dry with paper towels, then stack in piles for later. Using the large holes of a grater, grate the onion, mushrooms, carrot, zucchini and 2 tomatoes, keeping them separate for now. Heat 3 tablespoons of oil in a wide pot and sauté the onion until golden. Add the mushrooms, carrot, zucchini and rice and sauté for 10 minutes or so. Add the grated tomato, parsley, mint and lemon juice and season with salt and black pepper. Simmer for 5 minutes. Remove from the heat and stir in the kefalotiri.

Preheat the oven to 350°F. Spread a few whole vine leaves at a time on your work surface, shiny side down. Spoon a heaped tablespoon of filling onto each leaf and roll up neatly and snugly, tucking in the sides after the first roll and continuing to roll. Line them up in a large baking dish. They should just fit but if not, stack the last few on top. Grate the remaining tomato (so that the skin stays behind in your hand) and scatter it over the top of the dolmades. Add 1 cup of water and drizzle over the remaining oil. Sprinkle with salt and pepper. Rock the dish 2 or 3 times to distribute the liquid. Cover with foil. Bake for 1 hour, uncover and bake for 10 minutes or so.

HALVA TIS NIKOKIRAS HOUSEWIVES' HALVA

Χαλβάς

SERVES AN EXTENDED FAMILY

SYRUP

2⅔ CUPS SUGAR

JUICE OF ½ LEMON

LONG STRIP OF LEMON RIND

1 CINNAMON STICK

3 WHOLE CLOVES

1 CUP OLIVE OIL

⅔ CUP ALMONDS, SKIN ON, COARSELY CHOPPED

1 CUP FINE SEMOLINA

1 CUP COARSE SEMOLINA

GROUND CINNAMON, FOR SERVING

This is great for fasting purposes before Easter. At other times butter can be used instead of the oil if you like. It's a rather unusual cake and Greeks appreciate it for what it is. I have received many puzzled expressions when serving it to non-Greeks. Housewives have a code for this recipe: 1 2 3 4. The 1 is for the cup of oil, 2 for the semolina, 3 for the sugar and 4 for the water. I have strayed slightly from the code here in terms of the sugar, which I use a little less of. You could also add a couple of tablespoons of rose or orange blossom water to the syrup once it's finished simmering.

For the syrup, put the sugar, lemon juice and rind, cinnamon stick and cloves into a pot with 4 cups of water and bring to a boil. Simmer for 10 minutes or so.

Warm the oil in a big heavy-bottomed pot. Add the almonds and cook over medium heat, stirring, until lightly toasted. Stir in the semolinas and dry-roast them too until a bit golden here and there, stirring constantly and taking care that it doesn't burn.

Lightly oil a 6-cup capacity savarin or ring pan. Scoop out the lemon rind and spices from the syrup, then gradually stir the syrup into the roasting semolina. Take care when you pour it in, as it will bubble and splash. Stir constantly over low heat until the liquid is all absorbed by the semolina and it comes away from the side of the pot. Remove from the heat and scrape into the pan. Flatten with the back of a soupspoon or spatula to push out any creases or small spaces. Let it cool for a few minutes, then ease the halva away from the sides of the pan in a few places using a thin knife. Quickly turn the pan over and unmold the halva onto a flat plate. Scatter with the ground cinnamon and cut into slivers to serve. You only need thin pieces.

Alternatively there is the beautiful marble-looking slab of halva, available in Greek food stores, which is called "the grocers' halva" (halva tou mpakali). Some are plain, others have nuts and some are in swirls alternating chocolate and plain halva. It is made of tahini and is very rich and nutritious and just small slivers can be carved off as a snack. As a dessert, the plain version is wonderful in a chunk or small slice served with a scattering of cinnamon and a squeeze of lemon. This is eaten throughout the year but more so during fasting times.

SKORDALIA GARLIC POTATO + OLIVE OIL MASH

Σκορδαλιά

MAKES A NICE BOWLFUL

1 POUND 5 OUNCES UNPEELED POTATOES

8 GARLIC CLOVES, PEELED

SALT

JUICE OF 2 LEMONS

ABOUT ¾ CUP OLIVE OIL

FRESHLY GROUND BLACK PEPPER

You have got to have nice fresh garlic here. Not old tired cloves, but ones that give you an apple-type crunch when you start chopping. I have also seen things like the garlic being roasted or blanched in some lemon juice to get rid of some of its knockdown properties, but it's not really the real thing. And although you might feel awful breath-wise after this, it's well worth it. (Plus haven't they always said that garlic gets rid of mosquitoes and is great against colds and flu? So just see this as preventative medicine; really you are just doing yourself ounces of good.)

Skordalia goes very well with other fried foods such as keftedes. If you are poaching some fish and happen to have some fish broth, stir in a few tablespoons of that instead of the water to thin it out and add flavor. "And this," said Kiria Fotini from the Stavros museum in Ithaka, the inflections in her voice showing her love for the island as she rattled away her skordalia tricks, "this," she emphasized again, slapping her hand down onto the table, "is the whole secret. The trick that many people don't know. It takes it to a different level entirely," she finished, then indicating a goblet from which Odysseus may have drunk.

If you like, you can even make a bowl of some extra cloves of garlic crushed to a pulp and covered with olive oil to serve to those who really want a tremendous amount, as some might find the 8 garlic cloves in here a bit conservative. This keeps well in the fridge, covered, for 5 to 6 days. The strength of the garlic mellows over this time.

Boil the potatoes in their skins in salted water until soft. While they are cooking, crush the garlic cloves with a little salt to a purée using a mortar and pestle. When the potatoes are just cool enough to handle, peel off their skins and pass the potatoes through a ricer into a tall bowl. Add the puréed garlic and pour in the lemon juice and olive oil. Beat briskly with a wooden spoon until amalgamated and smooth. Season well with salt and pepper to taste; it needs a good amount of salt to bring out the flavors. Stir in 3 tablespoons or so of hot water or better still, hot fish broth if you have any. Serve with the fried salt cod on page 68.

BAKALIAROS SKORDALIA FRIED SALT COD

Μπακαλιάρος σκορδαλιά

SERVES 4

4 PIECES (ABOUT 6½ OUNCES EACH) BONELESS SALT COD FILLET, SKIN ON

ALL-PURPOSE FLOUR, FOR COATING

LIGHT OLIVE OIL, FOR FRYING

FRESHLY GROUND BLACK PEPPER

LEMON QUARTERS, FOR SERVING

SKORDALIA (PAGE 66), FOR SERVING

You could also use other fresh white fish fillets here, which would of course have no need for soaking. (Remember to sprinkle some salt on those when serving, though.)

The salt cod will need soaking for 2 to 3 days, and even then you should taste a small piece to see that it's not too salty before frying (the thinner tail end will be the saltiest part). It is also possible to get already soaked cod in some places.

People make this at home on March 25th, but many also go out to a restaurant. I ate it in a restaurant that served only these things: fried salt cod with skordalia, a plate of black-eyed peas, fava and a dish of olives, and then there was only halva for dessert. There was nothing else on the menu. Wine came from a barrel downstairs —what a restaurant!

To prepare the salt cod, put it in a bowl and cover with plenty of cold water. Cover the bowl with plastic wrap and refrigerate for 2 to 3 days, changing the water twice a day. You can taste a tiny piece to check whether it's too salty. If it is, you need to soak it for longer in fresh water. Rinse the fillets and dry well with paper towels. Put the flour in a deep plate and fill a deep bowl with cold water.

Add enough olive oil to a large skillet to come halfway up the sides of the fish. Heat the oil over medium-high heat until a cube of bread dropped in the oil browns in 15 seconds. Pat the fillets in the flour, coating both sides. Quickly dip them in the cold water, let the excess drip off, then pat in the flour again. Fry, skin side down, and when that is crisp, golden and firm, turn them over and do the other side. Drain on paper towels. Serve with a grinding of pepper and lemon quarters and a good dollop of skordalia on the side.

FASTING

F O O D S

There is grand security, I find, in Greece, in the presence of priests—and being physically near them. I love to be, for example, traveling with a priest or two on a boat. And if by chance the boat about to leave is suddenly canceled, I would definitely say it was for the better.

FAVA PURÉED YELLOW SPLIT PEAS

Φάβα

MAKES 4 CUPS

1 POUND 2 OUNCES
YELLOW SPLIT PEAS

1 SMALL RED ONION,
PEELED

2 GARLIC CLOVES, PEELED

ABOUT 1½ TEASPOONS
SALT

OLIVE OIL, FOR SERVING

1 LARGE RED ONION,
SLICED, FOR SERVING

HANDFUL OF CAPERS
WITH LEAVES, FOR
SERVING

FRESHLY GROUND BLACK
PEPPER

In Greece, fava refers to dried yellow split peas that, when boiled, melt into a creamy purée. This is great splashed with olive oil, pepper, capers and chunks of sweet red onions. It can be served as a meze with bread and cheese. It also works beautifully next to a main course, for example with grilled lamb cutlets. It is very easy to make; you could really just follow the instructions on the package you buy. If you have made it beforehand, you will need to add some water and heat it to thin out again to a soft, creamy mash, as it will have set in a clump.

Rinse the fava, then put into a pot and cover with cold water. Bring to a boil. Drain and give the fava a shower in a colander. Rinse out the pot, put the fava back in and add 4 cups hot water. Bring to a boil, add the whole onion and garlic and simmer, partly covered, for about 30 minutes. Remove the lid and simmer over low heat, stirring from time to time, for about 30 minutes more or until all the water has been absorbed and it starts glooping on the surface. Stir in the salt to taste. Discard the onion and garlic cloves and pulse the fava, with a hand-held blender if you have one, or in a food processor until smooth like soft mashed potato—much will have collapsed on its own and it may not even be necessary to purée. Leave it to sit for a bit, then spoon into a serving dish. Drizzle a good amount of olive oil over the top. Serve warm with the onion slices, capers and a grinding of pepper.

MAVROMATIKA BLACK-EYED PEAS (AND LENTILS)

Μαυρομάτικα (με φακές)

SERVES ABOUT 8

1¼ CUPS BLACK-EYED PEAS

1 SMALL RED ONION, PEELED

2 GARLIC CLOVES, PEELED

SALT

½ CUP BROWN LENTILS, RINSED AND DRAINED

6 TABLESPOONS OLIVE OIL, PLUS EXTRA FOR SERVING

3 TABLESPOONS RED WINE VINEGAR

1½ OUNCES GREEN ONIONS, CHOPPED

4 HEAPING TABLESPOONS COARSELY CHOPPED ITALIAN PARSLEY

2 TABLESPOONS COARSELY CHOPPED DILL

Often, plain boiled black-eyed peas are served crowded onto a small plate with a pile of chopped onions and parsley and a splashing of olive oil. This is just an all-mixed-in-together version with a couple of extra accessories.

It is wonderful served with a dish of feta, a dish of olives, a small dish of chopped tomatoes and some bread. Tuna works very well on the side, too.

Soak the beans in plenty of cold water overnight. Next day, drain and rinse them, then put into a pot and cover well with cold water. Bring to a boil. Drain and rinse out the pot. Give the beans a shower in a colander, then return to the pot with fresh water. Add the red onion and garlic cloves and bring to a boil, skimming the surface when necessary. Lower the heat and simmer for about 30 minutes. Add the lentils and simmer for another 30 minutes or so, until tender but not mushy. Add some salt in the last 5 to 10 minutes.

When done, drain the beans and lentils well through a fine sieve. Discard the onion and whole garlic cloves if you can find them. Put into a bowl to cool a bit.

Add the oil, vinegar, green onions, parsley and dill to the bowl and season with extra salt, if necessary, and a few grinds of pepper. Turn through very gently. Serve warm or at room temperature, with an extra drizzle of olive oil over individual servings.

TAHINOSOUPA
TAHINI SOUP

Ταχινόσουπα

SERVES 4

2 TEASPOONS SESAME
SEEDS

½ TEASPOON PAPRIKA

SPRINKLING OF GROUND
CHILE, OPTIONAL

1 TEASPOON GRATED
LEMON ZEST

ABOUT 5½ OUNCES FRESH
EGG-FREE NOODLES
(HILOPITES, PAGE 81), OR
2¾ OUNCES DRIED

½ CUP TAHINI

JUICE OF 1½ LEMONS

OLIVE OIL, FOR SERVING

FRESHLY GROUND BLACK
PEPPER

This is a very simple soup that can be made in minutes. Traditionally it's from the Cycladic Islands and is eaten in the week leading up to Easter, or on Good Friday, when simple meat-free foods are eaten.

Toast the sesame seeds lightly in a small dry skillet. Add the paprika and the chile, if using, and cook briefly, taking care not to burn it. Stir in the lemon zest and transfer to a small bowl.

Bring 4 cups of water to a boil in a pot with some salt.

Add the hilopites and boil until just tender, about 2 minutes, or according to the package instructions if dried.

Meanwhile, put the tahini and lemon juice into a bowl, add a ladleful of the boiling hilopites water and whisk until smooth. When the hilopites are ready, pour the tahini mixture in and stir gently over the heat for a couple of minutes. Taste for salt. Serve in bowls with a drizzle of olive oil, a scattering of the sesame-paprika mixture and a grind of pepper.

HILOPITES NOODLES

Χυλοπίτες

MAKES ABOUT 5½ OUNCES

²/₃ CUP ALL-PURPOSE
FLOUR

3 TEASPOONS OLIVE OIL

Hilopites are Greek-style noodles/pasta that are served on the side of some dishes or in soups. They are available dried in packages from Greek grocers, or you can make your own. These egg-free hilopites are good for the fasting period.

Stir the flour with a pinch of salt into a bowl. Add the olive oil and about 1½ tablespoons of water and mix into a loose dough with a wooden spoon. Now bring it together with your hands and knead for 1 to 2 minutes, adding a little more flour if necessary to give a smooth, quite dry dough. Rest at room temperature, covered loosely with a dish towel, for 30 minutes or so. Roll out very thinly, until almost see-through, on a dry surface that has been only very lightly floured. Cut into strips about ¾ inch wide, then cut those up into rough rectangles 1¼ to 1½ inches long. The hilopites can be left out to dry a little for easier handling (they will be less likely to stick together) for 30 minutes or so, but it's not necessary. If you try to completely dry long strands, they will tend to break into smaller lengths, but for the tahinosoupa (page 78) it is not a problem.

SOUPIES ME HORTA SQUID WITH GREENS

Σουπιές με χόρτα

SERVES 4

1 POUND 14 OUNCES SMALL–MEDIUM SQUID

14 OUNCES TRIMMED GREENS, CHOPPED INTO LARGE PIECES

¼ CUP OLIVE OIL

3 GARLIC CLOVES, CHOPPED

GOOD PINCH OF GROUND RED CHILE

1 CUP CANNED DICED TOMATOES

SALT AND FRESHLY GROUND BLACK PEPPER

½ CUP WHITE WINE

This is good made with spinach, swiss chard, Belgian endive, mustard greens or a couple of these in combination. It is healthy and really a dish based just on its ingredients—what you put in is exactly what you will get in flavor. The chunks of greens work well with the chunks of squid. You could use calamari—it wouldn't need as long to cook and would be more delicate.

Cut the heads off and pull the innards from the squid. Pull the quills out of the bodies. Cut off the tentacles just above the eyes. Rinse the bodies and tentacles in cold water and dry them on paper towels. Slice the bodies open, lay them flat and cut into large slices or chunks.

Rinse the greens and keep in a colander. Heat the oil and garlic in a nonstick skillet until you can smell the garlic. Add the squid and sauté on a high heat for a few minutes. Add the chile and tomatoes, cook for a few minutes to soften, then add some salt and pepper and the wine. When much of the wine has evaporated, add ½ cup of water. Cover, lower the heat and simmer for 15 to 20 minutes, or until the squid is tender when you poke a piece with a fork.

Add the greens to the squid with about 1 cup of water and bring back to bubbling. Season with a little salt, cover and simmer for 12 to 15 minutes—the greens should be softened and there should be a nice amount of reduced sauce to hold the dish together.

HTAPODI ME KOFTO MAKARONAKI OCTOPUS WITH SHORT PASTA

Χταπόδι με κοφτό μακαρονάκι

SERVES 4 TO 6

1 MEDIUM OCTOPUS (ABOUT 1¾ POUND)

5 TABLESPOONS OLIVE OIL

1 RED ONION, CHOPPED

½ TEASPOON PAPRIKA

2 GARLIC CLOVES, CHOPPED

1 BAY LEAF

PINCH OF GROUND CHILE

½ CUP RED WINE

14-OUNCE CAN CRUSHED TOMATOES

2 TABLESPOONS CHOPPED ITALIAN PARSLEY

SALT AND FRESHLY GROUND BLACK PEPPER

9 OUNCES SHORT PASTA, SUCH AS DITALINI

2 TABLESPOONS COARSELY CHOPPED ITALIAN PARSLEY, FOR SERVING

Here the octopus is baked, and then the just-boiled pasta is mixed through to produce a single tasty dish. You can also use a small rice-shaped pasta such as risoni or orzo, or even just a heap of spaghetti on the side is lovely.

To prepare the octopus, cut the tentacles off just below the eyes. Push the beak out from the center of the tentacles and cut the hard eyes from the head. Cut the head up one side, being careful to avoid the ink sac, and scrape out the innards. Rinse under cold running water and pat dry with paper towels. Cut the tentacles diagonally into 1½- to 2-inch lengths, and slice the body into similar-size pieces.

Preheat the oven to 350°F. Heat the oil in a large skillet and sauté the onion until softened.

Add the octopus, paprika, garlic, bay leaf and chile and cook until the octopus brightens in color and turns purpley. Add the wine, bring to a boil, reduce heat to low and simmer for 10 minutes or so. Add the tomatoes, parsley, and salt and pepper and bring back to the bubbling point. Scrape into a roasting pan of about 8½ × 12 inches. Bake in the oven for 45 minutes or so, checking once or twice that there is enough liquid. If needed, add a little hot water to keep the sauce thick but loose.

Meanwhile, cook the pasta in boiling salted water until tender. Drain. Add to the octopus dish and mix through. Serve scattered with the extra parsley and black pepper.

SPANAKORIZO SPINACH RICE

Σπανακόριζο

2¼ POUND SPINACH, RINSED AND DRAINED

4 TABLESPOONS OLIVE OIL

3½ OUNCES GREEN ONIONS WITH SOME GREEN, CHOPPED

3 TABLESPOONS CHOPPED DILL

1 CUP MEDIUM-GRAIN RICE

SALT

JUICE OF 1 SMALL LEMON

FRESHLY GROUND BLACK PEPPER

1 TABLESPOON CHOPPED MINT

I love putting such amounts of green stuff into a pot. Makes me feel like I am on the right track. You will need a big wide pot here. Choose lovely small spinach where you hardly have to discard any tough stalks. I have added some mint here to the traditional recipe. I love this with lots of lemon squeezed over, and pepper, and with a good dollop of yogurt on the side (page 131, made without any of the spices).

Coarsely chop the spinach leaves. Heat the olive oil in a very large pot and sauté the onions until pale gold and softened. Add the dill and sauté for 30 seconds or so then stir in the rice.

Now add the spinach. You might feel that it won't all fit in the pot, but fit in as much as you can. Add 2 cups of hot water and press down and turn the spinach until it begins to wilt and it's all in. Add a good amount of salt, turn the spinach over with a wooden spoon and put the lid on. Bring to a boil then turn through again. Lower the heat and simmer, covered, for about 15 minutes. If there is still water in the bottom of the pot toward the end of this time, take the lid off and turn up the heat to let it evaporate. Remove from the heat. Sprinkle in the lemon juice and add a few grinds of pepper. Turn through gently and taste for salt. Add the mint. Cover with a clean dish cloth, put the lid back on and leave for 10 minutes to steam. Serve hot or even at room temperature.

MIDOPILAFO
MUSSEL RICE

Μυδοπίλαφο

SERVES 4 TO 6

3 POUNDS 5 OUNCES BLACK MUSSELS, NOT TOO BIG

6 TABLESPOONS OLIVE OIL

3 GARLIC CLOVES, 1 WHOLE, 2 CHOPPED

2 THICK ITALIAN PARSLEY STALKS WITH LEAVES

½ CUP WHITE WINE

6½ OUNCES GREEN ONIONS, CHOPPED WITH SOME GREEN ALSO

¼ CUP COARSELY CHOPPED DILL, PLUS EXTRA, CHOPPED, FOR SERVING

3 TABLESPOONS OUZO

2 TOMATOES, GRATED ON THE LARGE HOLES OF A GRATER (SO THAT THE SKIN STAYS BEHIND IN YOUR HAND)

2 CUPS MEDIUM-GRAIN RICE

SALT

This is often made with all the shells removed, so if you prefer you can make it that way too (I love the shells). This is a dish from northern Greece, which is best served warm just after you have made it. It is great alone or along with other fish plates as part of a meze. Choose lovely fresh mussels. Nice with ouzo on ice.

Debeard the mussels and scrub them clean with a wire brush under running water. Drain. Give each one a tap and discard those that stay open. Heat 2 tablespoons of the oil in a high-sided pot large enough to hold all the mussels. Add the whole garlic and when it starts to smell good, add the drained mussels, parsley and wine. Put over high heat and cook, covered, until the mussels have opened. Remove the opened ones and give the others another chance. Remove from the heat and strain, keeping the liquid. Now discard any mussels that have not opened. When cool enough to handle, remove half of the mussels from their shells. Discard the empty shells and put the mussels together with the other ones still in their shells.

Heat the rest of the oil in a wide nonstick pot. Add the onion and sauté on low heat until soft and golden. Stir in the chopped garlic and half the dill and when they smell good, add the ouzo. Cook until it evaporates, then add the tomatoes. Increase the heat to medium and simmer for a few minutes, then add the rice, turning it through to coat well. Make the mussel broth up to 4 cups with hot water and add this to the pot with a little salt. Bring to a boil, lower the heat and simmer for 10 to 12 minutes,

continued

or until a lot of the liquid has been absorbed. Taste, adding salt if necessary. Add all the mussels, shelled and unshelled, turn through with a wooden spoon and simmer for another 5 minutes, checking that nothing sticks to the bottom of the pot. Remove from the heat, add the remaining dill and fluff up the rice. Cover the pot with a clean dish cloth. Put the lid back on and leave it for another 10 minutes or so to steam and finish cooking.

Serve with a grind of pepper and a scattering of the extra dill.

Many people will have been fasting up to the point of Easter Saturday. Many for as long as 40 days. First thing then on the Saturday morning, they will go (with nil by mouth) to take communion, then at 11:30 p.m. they will set off for the liturgy at church with their shiny shoes and their good clothes. Everyone has brought a lambada (a candle of natural wax), which must be lit from the holy light which works like this: every year a new light is lit in Jerusalem. The story goes that the patriarchis (head of the Orthodox church) goes down into the grave of Jesus holding a bunch of candles and by miraculous action the candles get lit. Up he comes with the candles to the representatives of all churches, and each one lights up and takes their candles back to their respective countries. The Greek one travels back by charter, and upon arrival in Athens a small fleet of helicopters and cars whiz off in various directions with their lighted candles. Priests can be seen then landing in helicopters outside major cathedrals to light the main candle before jetting off once more to light up other towns. Provincial priests are waiting at the cathedrals to light up and move on to their smaller churches, and so it goes until eventually the entire nation's candles are ablaze. This symbolically is the fotissi (enlightenment) of the people. When the priests in the churches give the light to all the people, everything starts to light up in a slow and steady ripple, until a whole country is shining. Then you know that the Greeks have got something special, because they have this faith—and I love them for their details. With their lit candles they go home well after midnight, many drawing a black cross with their candle flame under their doorframe to bless the house before entering. Then they crack their red eggs and whip the egg and lemon sauce into the lamb's intestine soup before eating it, and call it a day. (A foreigner alighting upon this scene slightly earlier may be surprised to find all tables set and not a soul in sight.) Next day comes the lamb on the spit, which can be seen turning in many corners of the country, and there will be many others roasting and grilling in different kitchens.

MAYIRITSA EASTER SOUP

Μαγειρίτσα

This lamb intestine and sikotaria soup is traditionally made and eaten after the Easter midnight mass. This is the recipe of Manos' mom, Aleka, which the family always makes. This is mostly prepared beforehand, then when everyone comes home from midnight mass, the egg and lemon sauce is whipped up as the last-minute preparation. A vegetarian mayiritsa is sometimes made using mushrooms.

SERVES ABOUT 8

1 LAMB SIKOTARIA OR INNARDS: LIVER, LUNGS AND OTHER ORGANS (ABOUT 2 POUNDS 10 OUNCES)

1 POUND 2 OUNCES LAMB INTESTINES

COARSE SALT, FOR RUBBING

1 LEMON, FOR CLEANING

2 TABLESPOONS BUTTER

2¾ OUNCES GREEN ONIONS, CHOPPED

1 CUP MEDIUM-GRAIN RICE

SALT AND FRESHLY GROUND BLACK PEPPER

1 LARGE HANDFUL CHOPPED DILL

7 MINT LEAVES

2 EGG YOLKS

JUICE OF 3 LEMONS

Put the innards in a large pot, cover with water and bring to a boil. Simmer for 20 minutes, skimming the surface of scum. Strain, reserving the broth. You will need about 4 cups for the soup. Cut the pluck into small irregular pieces.

Turn the intestines inside out with a skewer, rub with coarse salt and lemon to clean, then rinse and drain. If you don't turn them inside out, then cut into pieces. Cut the intestines into pieces of a similar size to the pluck. Rub between your hands with salt and lemon, then put in a bowl. Cover with water and leave for 10 minutes. Drain, rinse, then blanch in boiling water for 5 minutes. Rinse and drain.

Heat the butter in a large heavy-bottomed pot and sauté the onion until softened. Add the pluck and intestines. Fry for a minute or two, stirring, then add the reserved broth and 2 cups of water and bring to a boil. Add the rice, and season well with salt and pepper. Simmer, uncovered, on low heat for about 20 minutes, or until the meats are tender. Add the dill and mint and let it sit for a few minutes before serving. Remove the pot from the heat. Whisk the yolks and lemon juice in a bowl. Stir a little of the hot broth in to acclimatize it, then slowly stir the mixture back into the pot. Serve immediately.

2

TSOUREKI BRAIDED EASTER BREAD

Τσουρέκι

SERVES A FAMILY & FRIENDS

1 OUNCE FRESH YEAST, OR
1 TABLESPOON ACTIVE DRY
YEAST

⅔ CUP SUGAR, PLUS EXTRA
FOR DUSTING

¾ CUP LUKEWARM MILK

6¼ CUPS ALL-PURPOSE
FLOUR

½ TEASPOON MASTICHA
GRANULES

½ TEASPOON FRESHLY
GRATED NUTMEG

2 TEASPOONS ANISE SEEDS,
TOASTED AND GROUND

¼ TEASPOON SALT

½ CUP (1 STICK) BUTTER,
MELTED

2 EGGS, LIGHTLY BEATEN,
PLUS 1 EXTRA, BEATEN, FOR
BRUSHING

2 TABLESPOONS BRANDY

1 RED EGG (PAGE 104),
OPTIONAL

A red egg is set into the top of the braid before baking. Different spices are often used in this bread, and flaked almonds are sometimes scattered on top before baking. Many people like it just plain. Here there is masticha (ground resin from the masticha tree). You can leave it out for a plainer taste if you prefer. If possible, get the whole anise seeds here and grind them yourself for the lovely smell. Tsoureki is enjoyed for breakfast also and is lovely toasted and buttered.

Crumble or scatter the yeast into a wide basin. Sneak a teaspoon of sugar from your amount and add to the yeast, and pour in the milk. Whisk in 3 handfuls of the flour to give a smooth batter. Cover with a dish cloth and leave for half an hour or so in a warm place to activate and bubble up.

Grind the masticha with a teaspoon or so of the sugar to a powder. Mix the nutmeg, anise, masticha, sugar and salt into the remaining flour and add to the batter. Add the butter, 2 eggs and brandy. Mix it first with a wooden spoon, then change to your hands when a loose dough forms. Remove your rings (remember where you have put them!) and start kneading. Knead for 6 to 7 minutes, until you have a lovely smooth and spongy dough. Add more flour if necessary to give a firm dough. Wipe out the bowl with oiled paper towels. Put the dough in, cover with plastic wrap, then the dish cloth, and put another cloth on as well. Put in a warm place for about 2 hours, until it has puffed up to double its size.

Punch the dough down and knead it a couple of times. Separate it into three equal portions, weighing them if necessary. Gently stretch, tease and roll each into long ropes of about 14¼ inches. Line them up side by side on your work surface and press three ends together. Now braid them tightly and evenly, finishing with the tail ends pressed together and twisted underneath. Put onto a baking sheet lined with parchment paper, pressing in the two ends of the braid like you're playing an accordion to give a loaf 11¼ inches long. Cover loosely with a dish cloth and return to the warm spot until risen again, about 1 hour.

Preheat the oven to 350°F. Brush the top of the loaf with the extra egg and scatter the extra sugar over. Now nestle the red egg into the folds of the bread at one end. Bake until golden and it sounds hollow when tapped, 25 to 30 minutes. Cool on a wire rack before serving.

PASKALINA AVGA RED EGGS

Πασχαλινά (Κόκκινα) αυγά

MAKES 12 RED EGGS

12 EGGS

½ TEASPOON RED
POWDERED EGG
DYE, CHEMICAL-FREE
IF POSSIBLE

½ CUP WHITE WINE VINEGAR

OLIVE OIL, FOR POLISHING

Part of the Easter preparations is the dyeing of eggs. Mainly red, to represent the blood of Christ, but sometimes people use other colors. The eggs are polished with a drop of olive oil to make them lovely and shiny. These are sitting pretty in their baskets, just waiting to be cracked. The tradition is that you have to crack eggs after church and on Easter Sunday, and you must crack tops to tops and bottoms to bottoms with another contestant. The strongest egg wins. Over the next day or so they are peeled and cut into wedges and splashed with vinegar, olive oil, salt, pepper and paprika. One or more unpeeled ones will have been set into the tsoureki to bake. Even if they are overboiled and graying and bleeding dye, everyone loves the eggs and eats them after cracking.

Lower the eggs gently into a pot where they will fit close together in a single layer. Cover with water (room temperature). Bring slowly to a boil so that they don't bounce and crack. Simmer for a few minutes, then turn off the heat and leave them in the water for 10 minutes or so to cool and finish cooking. Drain.

Dissolve the dye in a cup of hot water. Put 2 cups of water (room temperature) and the vinegar in a bowl large enough to take 6 eggs with room between them. Stir in the dye and lower half the eggs in. If needed, add enough water to cover the eggs, making sure no tips or tops are sticking out. Leave for 2 to 3 minutes, rolling them around with a spoon once or twice so that the same part of them isn't always touching the bottom of the dish. Scoop out with a slotted spoon and drain on a plate lined with paper towels. Repeat with the remaining eggs.

As they are drying, roll the eggs over on the paper towels so that the undersides dry too. When they are all dry, polish with a paper towel dipped in olive oil. The dye will wash off plates and bowls, but might need a little scrubbing if you get some on your hands, so use gloves if you prefer.

I PALIA I KOTA EHI TO ZOUMI — THE OLD HEN HAS THE BROTH

ARNI LEMONATO LEMON + OREGANO LAMB

Αρνί λεμονάτο

SERVES 4 TO 6

1½ CUPS FRESH LEMON JUICE (6 TO 7 LEMONS)

½ CUP OLIVE OIL

1 HEAPING TABLESPOON DRIED OREGANO

3 POUNDS 5 OUNCES LEG OF LAMB, BONE HACKED IN ONE PLACE AND HINGED, SO IT FITS IN THE DISH

SALT AND FRESHLY GROUND BLACK PEPPER

2 POUNDS 10 OUNCES POTATOES, CUT INTO BIG CHUNKS

This is sooooo lemony. It is also a dish that you can really leave in the oven and go out shopping for a while and hardly even think about the fact that you left something in the oven.

This recipe is my friend Marion's way. She says to keep turning the lamb while it's marinating and spooning some of the marinade over every waking hour or so—she did say not to worry about it while sleeping. I use a large round (about 13 inches in diameter) or rectangular roasting pan here. You may have to ask your butcher to hack once into the leg (so it fits in the pan).

Mix the lemon juice, olive oil and oregano with 1½ cups of water in a large nonreactive baking dish. Rub the lamb well all over with salt and black pepper and put it in the marinade. Turn it over a couple of times to coat well. Cover with plastic wrap and refrigerate for 24 hours, turning it frequently throughout your waking hours.

Preheat the oven to 350°F. Transfer lamb and marinade to a roasting pan and cover the lamb with a sheet of parchment paper, and then cover the pan tightly with 3 layers of aluminum foil. Bake for 1 hour. Turn the lamb over, cover again and reduce the heat to 300°F. Bake the lamb for another 2 hours. Now turn the lamb gently, as it will be very tender. Add the potatoes to the dish and sprinkle a little salt over them. Cover again and bake for 2 hours, turning the potatoes once during this time. Remove the foil, shuffle the potatoes and put back in the oven at 400°F. Roast until a little golden here and there, 20 to 30 minutes. Remove from the oven and let the lamb rest for 5 minutes before serving.

GALAKTOBOUREKO CUSTARD PHYLLO PIE

Γαλακτομπούρεκο

SERVES 12

SYRUP

1½ CUPS SUGAR

1 LONG STRIP OF LEMON PEEL

FILLING

1¼ CUPS SUGAR

7 TABLESPOONS FINE SEMOLINA

2 TABLESPOONS PLUS 1 TEASPOON CORNSTARCH

4 EGG YOLKS, PLUS 2 WHOLE EGGS

6 CUPS MILK

2 TEASPOONS VANILLA EXTRACT

A NICE GRATING OF FRESH NUTMEG

12 SHEETS PHYLLO*, AT LEAST 12 X 15 INCHES IN SIZE

½ CUP (1 STICK) BUTTER, MELTED TO GOLDEN

This is my friend Annette's recipe. She is very good with desserts. I love the pureness of this pie. Syrupy Greek sweets are always served with a glass of cold water. Greeks have always loved making an outing to a café or zaharoplasteio (confectioners) to have a sweet. This is often the type of sweet you will find served after Easter lamb.

The butter should be heated and melted to a nice golden caramelly color for good flavor, and while you are making this, you will probably have to put the butter back onto the stove to melt again when it hardens a bit.

To make the syrup, put the sugar, lemon peel and ¾ cup of water in a saucepan over medium heat and stir until the sugar dissolves. Bring to a boil and simmer for about 5 minutes. Remove from the heat and cool. Preheat the oven to 325°F.

For the filling, put the sugar, semolina and cornstarch in the bowl of an electric mixer. Add all the eggs and beat until thick and pale. Heat the milk, vanilla and nutmeg in a large saucepan to just below boiling. Add a ladleful to the eggs and mix in. Add another ladleful, mix, and continue until all the milk has been added. Scrape back into the pot and return it to the heat on low for 5 to 10 minutes, whisking often until it is very thick and nothing sticks to the bottom. When it's thickened and gloopy and is just at the point before boiling, remove from the heat.

Have the phyllo sheets ready, covered by a dish cloth to prevent them drying out. Brush the base and sides of an 8½ × 12-inch baking dish with butter. Lay 1 sheet of phyllo on your work surface and brush with butter. Cover with another sheet, brush it with butter and continue in this way until you have a stack of 6 sheets. Lift them up and fit into the buttered dish, covering the base and sides. Press them gently into the corners of the dish to make a nest for the filling. Pour the filling on top and smooth the surface.

Make another stack of 6 buttered phyllo sheets. Lift this onto the pie, covering the filling. Press the two overhanging layers of phyllo together, trimming these to about an inch. Roll these edges over on themselves to seal the filling in. Using a sharp knife, gently score the top pastry into 12 pieces, only cutting through the top sheet or two of phyllo. Flick a little cold water here and there (to prevent the phyllo from curling). Bake until crisp and golden, about 25 minutes. Remove from the oven, let rest for a couple of minutes then pour the syrup over the top, covering all the pie. Now leave for at least 1 hour before serving to allow the syrup to settle as the pie cools.

Will keep for a number of days if left, covered with a dish cloth, in a cool, dry place (not refrigerated).

* *The phyllo sheets need to be large enough to cover the base and sides of an 8½ × 12-inch baking dish. If yours are smaller, use more sheets and cut to fit.*

MEZEDES

SHARED FOODS

The Greeks seem to have inherited such a natural sense of community. An ease of hospitality through which young and old move so easily. They can attach on new and sudden situations or people so smoothly—as though all of life were just one long Greek dance. And grandparents, babies and friends and relatives of every generation are sharing plates of appetizers on long tables.

SAGANAKI FRIED CHEESE

Σαγανάκι

SERVES 4

LIGHT OLIVE OIL,
FOR FRYING

1 EGG, LIGHTLY BEATEN

ALL-PURPOSE FLOUR,
FOR COATING

4¼-OUNCE, ¾-INCH-THICK
SLICE KASSERI-STYLE
CHEESE, OR TALAGANI

LEMON QUARTERS,
FOR SERVING

There is a typical pan called a saganaki, which is used for cooking and serving this—a small pan with handles on either side. You can use kasseri, kefalotiri or a softer type of Greek cheese such as talagani, which is my favorite for this savory version. Serve hot with lemon on the side for squeezing over.

Pour olive oil into a small non-stick skillet to a depth of roughly ½ inch.

Put the egg in one flat bowl and the flour in another. Heat the oil over medium-high heat until a cube of bread dropped in the oil browns in 15 seconds.

Dip the cheese slice in the egg, then pat it in the flour to coat well. Put the slice into the oil and fry until golden on both sides. Splash its sides with oil to make sure that they are fried golden, too. The cheese must be crisp on the outside and softened on the inside. When done, remove the cheese from the pan with tongs and drain on paper towels. Serve hot, cut up into squares and with lemon juice squeezed over the top. If serving in the pan, remove the cheese, pour away the oil, wipe the pan with a paper towel, return the cheese to the pan and squeeze some lemon over.

SAGANAKI WITH HONEY + SESAME

Σαγανάκι με μέλι και σουσάμι

SERVES 4

2 TABLESPOONS
MILD HONEY

4¼-OUNCE, ¾-INCH-THICK
SLICE KASSERI CHEESE
OR SIMILAR

1 EGG, LIGHTLY BEATEN

ALL-PURPOSE FLOUR,
FOR COATING

LIGHT OLIVE OIL,
FOR FRYING

1 TEASPOON BLACK
SESAME SEEDS

This sweet saganaki seems to work better with a stronger cheese, so rather kasseri than talagani. This is also served as an appetizer and is a nice surprise among other savory dishes, or just alone with a salad. I ate it on the island of Naxos.

Put the honey in a small briki (Greek coffee pot) or small saucepan and heat gently. Keep warm over a low heat.

Make the saganaki following the recipe on page 118. Serve the cheese with some warm honey drizzled over and the sesame seeds sprinkled on top. Nice with bread, too.

KEFTEDES FRIED MEATBALLS

Κεφτέδες

MAKES ABOUT 35

10½ OUNCES UNPEELED POTATOES (ABOUT 2)

1 POUND 2 OUNCES GROUND BEEF

1 RED ONION, GRATED

2 TABLESPOONS COARSELY CHOPPED ITALIAN PARSLEY

1 TEASPOON DRIED OREGANO

1 TEASPOON DRIED MINT

GOOD PINCH OF GROUND CINNAMON

1 EGG, LIGHTLY BEATEN

SALT AND FRESHLY GROUND BLACK PEPPER

ALL-PURPOSE FLOUR, FOR DUSTING

OLIVE OIL, FOR FRYING

LEMON QUARTERS, FOR SERVING

These are very popular in Greece. They are lovely as a meze with a dish of feta and a few other bits and pieces. Of course they are also great with french fries. Many Greeks roll their keftedes in a little flour before frying.

Boil the potatoes, covered, in plenty of water until they are soft when pierced with a fork.

Meanwhile, put the beef, onion, parsley, oregano, mint, cinnamon and egg into a bowl and mix. Drain the cooked potatoes and when they are cool enough to handle, peel and break up into the bowl. Season well with salt and pepper, then mash everything together with a potato masher. Knead again with your hands to make a compact mix. Form walnut-size balls of about 1 ounce each, but you can make them smaller or bigger if you like. Scatter some flour onto a flat plate and roll the balls lightly in the flour, keeping them in compact balls.

Heat olive oil to a depth of about ¼ inch in a large nonstick skillet. Add as many balls as will fit to the skillet and fry until they are golden on all sides, flicking them gently to roll over. You will probably have to fry in two batches. Remove carefully with tongs and drain on a plate lined with paper towels. Add a little salt (as fried things are always good with a last sprinkling of salt). Serve hot, with a few drops of lemon juice.

REVITHOKEFTEDES CHICKPEA BALLS

Ρεβυθοκεφτέδες

MAKES 18

½ CUP DRIED CHICKPEAS

1 TABLESPOON ALL-PURPOSE FLOUR, PLUS EXTRA FOR COATING

6½ OUNCES POTATO (1 MEDIUM–LARGE)

¼ CUP ONION, GRATED ON THE LARGE HOLES OF A GRATER

1 TABLESPOON COARSELY CHOPPED DILL

1 TABLESPOON COARSELY CHOPPED ITALIAN PARSLEY

SALT AND FRESHLY GROUND BLACK PEPPER

LIGHT OLIVE OIL, FOR FRYING

LEMON QUARTERS, FOR SERVING

These are everywhere on the island of Sifnos and go well on any table with anything, anywhere, at any time. The chickpeas are not cooked here, only soaked overnight and then pulsed to a purée in a food processor. Leave a little texture in them, though.

Soak the chickpeas and the flour in plenty of cold water overnight.

Boil the potato in salted water until very tender. Drain. When cool enough to handle, peel and mash with a fork in a large bowl. Drain the soaked chickpeas and purée them, leaving some texture. Add to the potato along with the onion, dill and parsley. Season with salt and pepper and mix well. Shape 18 walnut-size balls of about 1 ounce each. Put some flour in a bowl and gently roll the balls in this to coat.

Pour the olive oil into a large skillet to a depth of ¼ inch and put over medium-high heat.

Fry the balls in batches, gently turning them to brown evenly. As they are done, remove with tongs and drain on paper towels. Sprinkle with salt and serve hot or cold with the lemon quarters.

TOMATOKEFTEDES FRIED TOMATO FRITTERS

Ντοματοκεφτέδες

MAKES ABOUT 15

10½ OUNCES LOVELY RIPE RED TOMATOES (ABOUT 3)

2½ OUNCES RED ONION, COARSELY CHOPPED (1 SMALL)

3 HEAPING TABLESPOONS COARSELY CHOPPED MINT

1⅔ CUPS ALL-PURPOSE FLOUR

SALT AND FRESHLY GROUND BLACK PEPPER

1 HEAPING TEASPOON BAKING POWDER

OLIVE OIL, FOR FRYING

These are everywhere on the island of Santorini. Santorini will offer you amazing tomatoes, fava, capers, wine, seafood, views, volcanoes . . . if you go slightly out of season, it is incredible. Some go just for the sunsets, dangling legs off walls toward the departing star and its spectacular performance. You may have to go there to get your tomatoes to make these lovely fried things. Alternatively, choose wonderful ripe red tomatoes. These fritters have lovely rough edges, with bits of tomato, mint and onion chunks sticking out of the sides that have crisped during the frying like hedgehogs.

Cut the top hats off the unpeeled tomatoes and discard. Slice the tomatoes into 6 wedges, then chop each wedge into 4 or 5 pieces. Scrape off the board into a bowl but leave behind the excess juice. Add the onion, mint and half the flour to the bowl. Season with salt and pepper and knead in well. Leave for 10 minutes or so to soften.

Make a paste with the remaining flour, the baking powder and ⅓ cup of water. Add to the bowl and mix in well. Heat olive oil to a depth of about ⅝ inch in a large nonstick skillet until very hot. Scoop up a good tablespoon of the mixture and with another spoon, scrape this into the hot oil in lovely irregular fritters. Fry a few at a time, turning them over when golden to fry the other side. Remove with a slotted spoon and drain on a plate lined with paper towels. Sprinkle with a little extra salt and serve on a clean plate.

KOLOKITHAKIA KE MELITZANES TIGANITES FRIED ZUCCHINI + EGGPLANT

Κολοκυθάκια και μελιτζάνες τηγανιτές

SERVES 3

7 OUNCES ZUCCHINI
(ABOUT 1)

7 OUNCES EGGPLANT
(ABOUT ½ AN EGGPLANT),
HALVED LENGTHWISE

ALL-PURPOSE FLOUR,
FOR COATING

LIGHT OLIVE OIL,
FOR FRYING

ALATOPIPERIGANO
(PAGE 128)

TZATZIKI (PAGE 130)

The wonderful thing I learned in Greece in the summer was this quick twice flouring and dipping in water method that produces a great crispier result. So have a bowl of flour and a bowl of cold water ready. It may seem like a bit of a fuss, but it's worth it. This is a beauty with tzatziki for dipping the fried vegetables into.

Cut the zucchini into slices about ⅛ inch thick. Cut the eggplant into half-moons about ⅛ inch thick. Put the flour onto a plate, and have a bowl of cold water ready.

Pour the olive oil into a large nonstick skillet to roughly ½ inch deep. Heat the oil over medium-high heat until a cube of bread dropped into the oil browns in 15 seconds. Pat slices of zucchini in flour to coat both sides. Shake off the excess, then dip the slices in the water. Shake a bit and pat well in flour again on both sides. Fry in batches until golden, turning them over and frying the other side, too. Don't overcrowd the pan and if they're cooking too quickly, turn the heat down. Remove the crisp and golden zucchini slices to a large plate lined with paper towels. Scatter them with alatopiperigano and get the next batch going. Once the zucchini are done, do the exact same thing with the eggplant. Serve hot, with tzatziki. These are also lovely with lemon.

ALATOPIPERIGANO
ALATI=SALT
PIPERI=PEPPER
RIGANI=OREGANO

Αλατοπιπερίγανο

1 TEASPOON SALT

2 TEASPOONS DRIED OREGANO

FEW GRINDS OF BLACK PEPPER

It is easy to scatter these ingredients over separately, but you can also mix them up to have ready for scattering over fried and grilled food. Needless to say, it's wonderful over french fries. Also with some grilled bread drizzled with olive oil and some of this, as a snack or on the side of any meal.

Mix all together and keep in an airtight container.

PATATES TIGANITES FRENCH FRIES

Πατάτες τηγανιτές

SERVES 2

10½ OUNCES LONG POTATOES (ABOUT 2)

LIGHT OLIVE OIL, FOR FRYING

ALATOPIPERIGANO (OPPOSITE)

This amount of french fries is just small enough to make a flat layer in the pan and not be too crowded and yet enough to make it worth the extra trouble of making them. They are great with tzatziki (page 130), and are also wonderful with some feta crumbled over them and then a crumbling of dried oregano. Fries in Greece are often served next to a main saucy dish with a scattering of shredded cheese over.

Peel the potatoes, halve them lengthwise and slice each half into 3 or 4 wedges. Put into a bowl of cold water with some salt and leave them for 30 minutes to 1 hour to soak off some of the starch. Drain well and pat dry with paper towels. Wrap in a clean dish cloth to dry further while the oil is heating.

Pour a good ½ inch depth of oil into a large skillet. Heat the oil over medium-high heat until a cube of bread dropped into the oil browns in 15 seconds. When you think it's hot enough, throw in a wedge to see if it bubbles and fizzles. If so, add all the wedges, leveling them so they are not on top of each other. When they start to look soft, poke at them with a wooden spoon to roughen up their surfaces. Leave them alone again until they start looking crunchy, then shuffle them with a wooden spoon, turning them if necessary. Turn the heat down if the oil bubbles too quickly and becomes too hot; you don't want dark brown, soggy chips. When they are light golden and crisp, move them around in the pan with a slotted spoon and remove to a plate lined with paper towels. Scatter with alatopiperigano. Serve at once.

TZATZIKI YOGURT, CUCUMBER, GARLIC

Τζατζίκι

MAKES A NICE BOWLFUL

2 GARLIC CLOVES

1 TABLESPOON OLIVE OIL

5¾ OUNCES CUCUMBER
(1 SMALL)

1 TEASPOON SALT

12 OUNCES GREEK YOGURT

1½ TABLESPOONS
CHOPPED MINT

FRESHLY GROUND BLACK
PEPPER

This is a subtle amount of garlic compared with some versions that you may come across. So you can add more if you like. If the garlic bothers you, you can leave it out completely, but it's not really tzatziki then. (And garlic is good for colds, plus it keeps vampires away.) See yogurt on the side (opposite) for a plainer version. Tzatziki is a beauty, as it takes just about anything to a different level. Wonderful with french fries, lamb cutlets, bread and many other dishes.

You can use 2 teaspoons or so of dried mint instead of fresh. If you prefer a milder garlic taste, then marinate the garlic in the oil and pour off the oil after without adding the garlic. If you are making regular tzatziki, then just make sure everyone within a 5-mile radius has some.

Using the flat of your knife, crush the garlic with a pinch of salt into a paste. Put into a small bowl with the oil and leave to marinate while you proceed with the rest.

Trim the cucumber and peel it. I like it striped, with one strip peeled and the next left unpeeled. Using the large holes of the grater, grate the cucumber into a sieve. Scatter with the salt and leave it for 30 minutes or so to drain, turning it over a couple of times and even pressing it down with your hands or a wooden spoon.

Put the yogurt into a bowl for serving. Add the garlic and oil, the mint and a couple of grinds of black pepper. Fold the cucumber through and taste for salt. This can be stored in the fridge, covered, for a couple of days. The cucumber will give up a little water, but stir it through to loosen the tzatziki.

YIAOURTI YOGURT ON THE SIDE

Γιαούρτι

SERVES 4 TO 6

1 GARLIC CLOVE, CRUSHED

1 TABLESPOON OLIVE OIL

1 CUP GREEK YOGURT

ABOUT ¼ CUP PLAIN YOGURT

A LARGE PINCH OF PAPRIKA

½ TEASPOON DRIED MINT

SALT AND FRESHLY GROUND BLACK PEPPER

Of course a good dollop of plain thick Greek yogurt, unfussed with, is also wonderful. For example, on a baked potato with a drizzling of olive oil and a scattering of salt and pepper.

This works very well in place of tzatziki for dishes where you may want something plainer. Depending on what you will be serving it with, you can leave out the mint and paprika.

Put the crushed garlic and the olive oil in a cup and leave to steep for half an hour or so.

Put the Greek yogurt in a bowl. Add just enough regular yogurt to loosen it (you might have some left over, as not all Greek yogurts are of the same thickness). Add the paprika and mint, and pour the olive oil in, keeping back the garlic clove. Season to taste with salt and black pepper and mix.

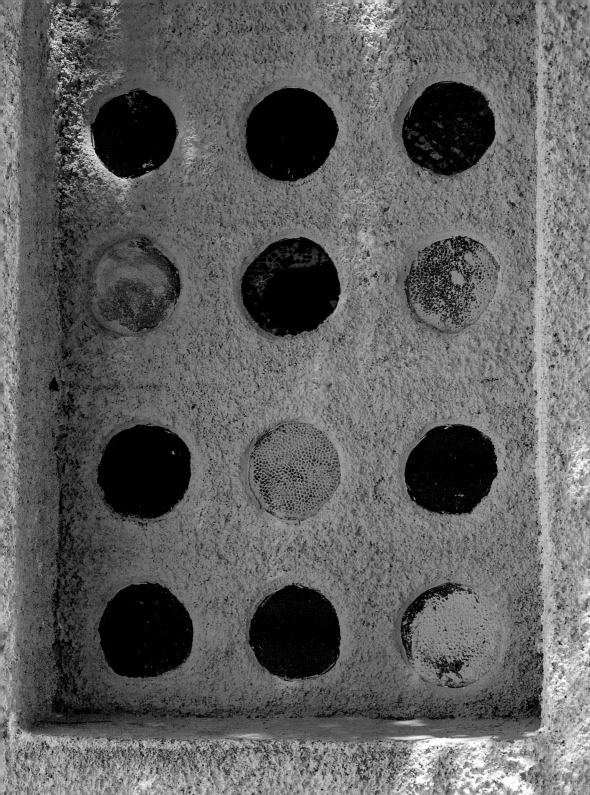

HTAPODI XIDATO VINEGARED OCTOPUS

Χταπόδι ξυδάτο

SERVES 4 TO 6

1 LARGE OCTOPUS (ABOUT 2 POUNDS 10 OUNCES)

6 TABLESPOONS OLIVE OIL

6 TABLESPOONS RED WINE VINEGAR

½ TEASPOON DRIED OREGANO

1 LARGE GARLIC CLOVE, CHOPPED

SALT AND FRESHLY GROUND BLACK PEPPER

This is a wonderful meze served with ouzo or raki.

There is a saying in some parts of Greece that says "the octopus separates the couple," as it appears so big initially and ends up so shrunken when cooked. Years ago when the husband saw the result after a hard day's work, he might have been furious with his wife that there was much less to eat than what had appeared in the uncooked state!

You will often see octopus catchers in Greece bashing their just-caught octopus against the rocks to tenderize it.

To prepare the octopus, slice about two-thirds of the way across, just below the eyes, keeping the tentacles still attached to the head. Scrape the innards out of the head, being careful not to puncture the ink sac. Cut the hard eyes from the head and push the beak out from the center of the tentacles. Rinse under cold running water and shake dry over the sink. Put whole into a heavy-bottomed pot with absolutely nothing else. Cover, put over the lowest possible heat and simmer gently for about 1¼ hours, turning it a couple of times. It should stew in its own juices, but if it is looking dry and beginning to stick to the pot, add a little hot water. By the end, the liquid will be almost jammy and the octopus should be very tender when poked with

HTAPODI SCHARA GRILLED OCTOPUS

Χταπόδι σχάρας

a fork. If not, add a little more water and continue cooking.

Remove the pot from the heat and set aside, still covered, while the octopus cools down. Remove the octopus from the pot and slice away the tentacles. Cut the tentacles up into easy-to-put-on-your-fork pieces, discarding any skin that comes away. Put into a bowl and add the olive oil, vinegar, oregano, garlic, pepper, and taste for salt. Mix together. It is important that you can taste the vinegar–that's the name of this dish. Cover with plastic wrap and leave in the fridge to marinate for a few hours, mixing it a couple of times, before serving.

A grilled octopus is equally excellent. Often these are cleaned and hung out in the sun to dry for a few hours. Sometimes they are boiled first to soften and then quickly grilled for flavor.

Prepare your octopus as opposite. Cut into 8 individual tentacles, and cut the head to open it out. Put the pieces in a wire grill rack and grill quickly over very hot coals, flipping them over when deep golden and charred here and there.

Cut up into good slices. Drizzle with olive oil, splash with red wine vinegar, crumble over some oregano and give a good grind of pepper. Serve with ouzo on ice.

GAVROS MARINATED ANCHOVIES

Γαύρος

SERVES 4 TO 6

10½ OUNCES GAVROS
(FRESH ANCHOVIES)

ABOUT ½ CUP WHITE
WINE VINEGAR

1 HEAPING TABLESPOON
CHOPPED ITALIAN PARSLEY

3 TABLESPOONS OLIVE OIL,
PLUS EXTRA FOR SERVING

2 GARLIC CLOVES, HALVED

1 TEASPOON DRIED
OREGANO

JUICE OF ½ LEMON

FRESHLY GROUND BLACK
PEPPER

You can add in some other herbs and spices here to take on a different flavor. This is great served with other fish meze like the vinegared octopus, and with some taramosalata and bread it can end up being the whole meal. The gavros will keep for 3 days or so, covered with plastic wrap in the fridge.

Cut the heads off the anchovies and run a small sharp knife down their bellies to open them. Pull out the innards and the skeleton with the tail attached. If they haven't parted already, pull apart the sides to make 2 individual fillets. Rinse, then pat dry with paper towels. Arrange the fillets skin side down in a nonreactive dish that is just large enough to take them in 2 layers. Pour in enough vinegar to cover the fillets. Cover with plastic wrap and leave in the fridge for 4 hours or so.

Take the fillets from the dish, shaking off excess vinegar. Layer them in a flattish bowl, salting a little in between layers as you go. Add the parsley, olive oil and garlic, and the oregano crushed between your fingers. Add the lemon juice and a few good grinds of pepper. Shuffle to distribute. Cover with plastic wrap and leave to mingle before eating them—a few hours is good, the next day is even better. Drizzle with the extra olive oil just before eating.

GARIDES SAGANAKI SHRIMP WITH FETA + TOMATO

Γαρίδες σαγανάκι

SERVES 6 TO 8

ABOUT 16 MEDIUM
RAW SHRIMP

5 TABLESPOONS OLIVE OIL

1¾ OUNCES GREEN ONIONS
WITH SOME GREEN, FINELY
CHOPPED

3 GARLIC CLOVES, CHOPPED

14-OUNCE CAN CRUSHED
TOMATOES

¼ CUP CHOPPED ITALIAN
PARSLEY

SALT AND FRESHLY GROUND
BLACK PEPPER

4½ OUNCES FETA,
CRUMBLED

I have seen these baked as well as made on the stovetop. This recipe has lovely strong, clean flavors, and it works well as a meze with other seafood dishes. You really just need some bread with it.

Here I have cleaned the shrimp, leaving the tail on, but you might decide to leave the shell on, just cutting down the back and deveining.

Peel the shrimp, leaving the tails intact, and devein them using a toothpick. Heat the oil in a wide nonstick pan that has a lid and sauté the onion on medium-low heat until softened. Add the garlic and fry until it smells good, then add the tomatoes, half the parsley and some salt and pepper. Put the lid on and simmer for 10 minutes or so.

Add the shrimp to the pan and turn through to cover all of them with sauce. Simmer, covered, for 3 to 4 minutes. Scatter the feta in, put the lid back on and cook until the feta just softens, about 5 minutes, rocking the pan once or twice. Serve with a good grind of pepper and the remaining parsley scattered on top, and some lovely Greek bread.

KALAMARI TIGANITO FRIED CALAMARI

Καλαμάρι τηγανιτό

SERVES 2

14 OUNCES SMALL–
MEDIUM CALAMARI

ALL-PURPOSE FLOUR,
FOR DUSTING

LIGHT OLIVE OIL,
FOR FRYING

ALATOPIPERIGANO
(PAGE 128), FOR SERVING

LEMON QUARTERS,
FOR SERVING, OPTIONAL

Please use lovely fresh and tender calamari here. It must be eaten with just a scattering of salt, pepper and oregano, and some lemon on the side for whoever would like. Have a bowl of plain flour and a bowl of water ready and your pan of oil heating up. Sometimes calamari splatters and pops in the skillet, so it's a good idea to have a splatter mat that you can cover the skillet with while the calamari is frying.

Cut the heads off and pull the innards from the calamari. Pull the transparent spine out of the body. Cut off the tentacles just above the eyes. Rinse the bodies and tentacles in cold water and dry them on paper towels. Slice the bodies into rings about 5/8 inch or as you like them. Keep the tentacles whole (unless they are big).

Put the flour on a deep plate, and pour cold water into a deep bowl. Pour olive oil to a depth of at least ½ inch into a skillet and put over high heat. Pat the calamari in the flour to coat well, shake off the excess, then quickly dip them in the cold water. Pat them again well in the flour and shake off lightly. Fry in batches in the hot oil, turning them once, until they are golden and crusty. Remove to a plate lined with paper towels to drain while frying the rest. Scatter with alatopiperigano and serve at once with lemon for those who would like it.

TIROKAFTERI SPICY FETA

Τυροκαυτερή

MAKES ABOUT 1 CUP

1 GARLIC CLOVE

2 TABLESPOONS OLIVE OIL

2 MILD GREEN CHILES
(ABOUT ¾ OUNCE EACH)

8¾ OUNCES FETA, BROKEN
INTO SMALLISH PIECES

OLIVE OIL, TO SERVE

A PINCH OR TWO OF
GROUND CHILE, ACCORDING
TO TASTE

This is great with koulouria bread rings (or regular bread or pita) as part of a meze or even just alone. I love it served before grilled lemon and oregano lamb cutlets with a plate of plain stewed green beans, a green salad and a dish of olives. Very fine. You can make it hotter or milder as you like—naturally this will depend on your chiles. Will keep in the fridge, covered, for 5 to 6 days.

Preheat the oven to the hottest it will go. Peel the garlic and bruise it with the flat of your knife and put it into a small bowl with the olive oil to steep. Trim and seed the chiles. It's a good idea to use disposable gloves for this, so the burning chile doesn't remain on your hands. Put them on a sheet of foil and dry-roast them in the oven for about 10 minutes, until soft and blistery. Chop them up finely, then put in a mortar or mini processor with a tablespoon of the oil and blend to a paste. Add the feta and pulse until all the lumps are gone.

Scrape into a bowl and stir in the olive oil (remove the garlic). Serve with a little olive oil drizzled over and a sprinkling of ground chile if you think it's not hot enough.

PIPERIES XIDATES MARINATED PEPPERS

Πιπεριές ξυδάτες

The lovely small sweet Greek peppers can be fried whole or grilled, their skins removed, then put in a dish to marinate with a little vinegar, salt and oregano, a clove of garlic and a splash of best olive oil. They are fantastic with mashed feta on bread and some olives. These will keep in the fridge, covered with plastic wrap, for a few days, but they are best eaten at room temperature.

CUCUMBER MEZE

Αγγουρομεζές

SERVES 2

7 OUNCES CUCUMBER (ABOUT 1), PEELED AND SLICED

JUICE OF ½ LEMON

½ TEASPOON DRIED MINT

SALT AND FRESHLY GROUND BLACK PEPPER

ABOUT 1 TABLESPOON OLIVE OIL

This is extremely instant and extremely simple. The kind of thing you could eat a bucket of in summer. The recipe is easy to double; just reduce the olive oil slightly, using about 1½ teaspoons.

Put the cucumber and lemon juice into a bowl and crumble in the mint. Add salt and pepper. Drizzle the olive oil over just before serving.

PIPERIES YEMISTES ME FETA
PEPPERS STUFFED WITH FETA

Πιπεριές (γεμιστές) με φέτα

SERVES 4

4 SMALL RED AND GREEN SWEET PEPPERS, ABOUT 1½ OUNCES EACH AND 4 INCHES LONG

7 OUNCES FETA

1 TABLESPOON OLIVE OIL

¼ TEASPOON DRIED OREGANO, OPTIONAL

Greek florinis, red peppers, are beautiful and sweet. And they also have pale green thin-fleshed ones, which are ideal for this dish. Very different in size from the large bell peppers available in many places. You will need something like the long thin ones, which weigh around 1½ ounces each. You could also use mizithra in place of the feta.

Cut the tops off the peppers and carefully remove the seeds, keeping the peppers whole. Crumble the feta and stuff tightly into the peppers, then replace the tops. Heat the olive oil in a skillet and sauté the peppers over high heat (propping the peppers up against the sides of the skillet so the filling doesn't ooze out), gently turning them over, until they are lightly browned on the outside, and the feta is melted a bit but not running out (the hats may fall off, but replace when serving). Serve whole or cut into thick slices, with the oregano crumbled over the top, if desired.

FETA FOURNOU BAKED FETA

Φέτα φούρνου

SERVES 2, OR 4 AS PART OF A MEZE

7 OUNCES FETA, CRUMBLED

1½ OUNCES GREEN SWEET PEPPER, FINELY SLICED (ABOUT 1 SMALL)

½ SMALL TOMATO, CHOPPED

1 TO 2 TABLESPOONS OLIVE OIL

2 GOOD PINCHES OF DRIED OREGANO

FRESHLY GROUND BLACK PEPPER

This is nice made in small individual ceramic dishes. Mine are flat and about 4¼ inches in diameter and 1¼ inches high. Serve hot with bread.

Preheat the oven to 400°F. Divide the feta between 2 small shallow ceramic dishes. Scatter the green pepper over the top and then the tomato over the pepper. Drizzle on the olive oil, crumble the oregano in and top with a good grind of black pepper. Bake until a bit crusty on the sides, about 20 minutes.

MELITZANOSALATA MASHED EGGPLANT

Μελιτζανοσαλάτα

SERVES 6

12 OUNCES EGGPLANT (ABOUT 1 LARGE EGGPLANT, PREFERABLY LONG, NOT ROUND)

2 TABLESPOONS OLIVE OIL

½ SMALL RED ONION, PEELED AND FINELY CHOPPED

1 GARLIC CLOVE, PEELED AND FINELY CHOPPED

1 SMALL TOMATO, PEELED AND CHOPPED, NOT TOO FINELY

2 TEASPOONS LEMON JUICE

¼ TEASPOON SWEET PAPRIKA

½ TEASPOON DRIED OREGANO

1 HEAPING TABLESPOON COARSELY CHOPPED ITALIAN PARSLEY

SALT AND FRESHLY GROUND BLACK PEPPER

If you have an outdoor grill going, then it is wonderful to grill your eggplant on it. If not, you can roast it at a high temperature in the oven to darken the skin in places and give it a lovely smoky roasted taste. It is important to dry out the eggplant to get the flesh soft and scrapable and not liquidy.

There are many different versions of this eggplant dish; some have vinegar rather than the lemon juice, others have yogurt. You could also add some fresh mint for a different journey. Lovely with pita as a meze or alone even. Or as a side next to a lamb dish.

Preheat a grill to hot. Rinse the eggplant, then prick it in a few places here and there with a fork so the skin won't burst while cooking. Put it on a rack 6 inches or so from the coals and grill for 40 to 50 minutes, turning a few times until softened, blackened and smoky. Set aside to cool slightly.

While the eggplant is cooking, heat the olive oil in a nonstick skillet over medium heat and sauté the onion until sticky and well cooked but not browned. Add the garlic and cook until you just smell it, then stir in the tomato. Simmer for 10 minutes or so, until the tomato has collapsed into a chunky sauce and you can see tomato frying in oil again. Remove from the heat.

Cut the stalk off the eggplant and halve the eggplant lengthwise. Squeeze out excess liquid over the sink. Using a pointed teaspoon, scrape out the flesh into a bowl and mash or chop it finely. Discard the skin. Add the tomato mixture and mash it roughly with a fork. Add the lemon juice, paprika and herbs and season with salt and pepper. Serve at room temperature.

MIDIA
MUSSELS WITH FETA + PEPPERS
Μύδια

ABOUT 3 POUNDS 5 OUNCES BLACK MUSSELS

5 TABLESPOONS OLIVE OIL

1 SMALL RED SWEET PEPPER (ABOUT 1½ OUNCES), SLICED INTO THIN RINGS

1 SMALL GREEN SWEET PEPPER (ABOUT 1½ OUNCES), SLICED INTO THIN RINGS

2 GARLIC CLOVES, CHOPPED

PINCH OF GROUND CHILE

JUICE OF 2 LEMONS

7 OUNCES FETA, COARSELY CHOPPED

¼ CUP CHOPPED ITALIAN PARSLEY

FRESHLY GROUND BLACK PEPPER

The Greek peppers are beautiful. Red and pale green. Small and long. Thin fleshed. A couple of them here sliced in rings give a great flavor. If you can't find those, then use a similar weight of other small sweet peppers.

This dish can also be served with the mussels shelled, but I love shells on. Make sure your mussels are fresh. Serve with bread.

Debeard the mussels. Scrub them with a wire brush under cold running water, then drain. Give each one a tap and discard those that stay open. Heat the oil in a pot large enough to take the mussels and that has a lid. Sauté the peppers until softened. Add the garlic and chile and when it smells good, add the mussels. Put the lid on, turn up the heat and cook just a minute or so, until the mussels open. Give the ones that haven't opened another chance to open, but then discard those that still have not opened. Add the lemon juice, put the lid back on and give the pot a shake.

Scatter the feta over the top, return the lid and shake the pot again. Leave for a minute for the feta to soften, but don't let it dissolve; it's nice to be able to see soft chunks of feta here and there. Add the parsley and a good few grinds of black pepper and stir gently. Serve hot.

OMELETA HORIATIKI POTATO, FETA + OREGANO OMELET

Ομελέτα χωριάτικη

SERVES 4

¼ CUP OLIVE OIL

10½ OUNCES POTATOES, PEELED, CUT INTO ⅛ INCH ROUNDS

1 TEASPOON DRIED OREGANO

3½ OUNCES FETA

6 EGGS, LIGHTLY BEATEN

FRESHLY GROUND BLACK PEPPER

This, served with bread and a salad, is a wonderfully simple supper. It is ideal if you can have the broiler on to finish cooking the large omelet by giving heat from the top, but if not, then just continue cooking it covered on low on the stovetop.

Heat the oil in a 12-inch nonstick skillet. Add the potatoes and fry gently on both sides until golden (but not too crisp) and completely cooked through. Salt lightly. Crumble the oregano over the potato with your fingers, then crumble the feta on top.

If you have a broiler, preheat it now. Pour the eggs into the skillet, shuffling gently so that they can leak down and around the potatoes. Put the lid on and cook over low heat until the eggs are set throughout but still runny on top. Keep an eye on the heat to ensure that the bottom doesn't burn but forms a golden crust. Take the lid off the skillet and place the skillet 4 inches or so under the broiler. If you aren't using a broiler, just keep the lid on the skillet and continue cooking the eggs slowly. When it's just slightly runny here and there, remove from the heat and leave it with the lid on for a couple of minutes. Loosen the edges and slide it out of the skillet upright onto a large serving plate. Serve hot, with a grind of black pepper.

STRAPATSADA SCRAMBLED EGGS WITH TOMATO

Στραπατσάδα

SERVES 3

2 TABLESPOONS OLIVE OIL

½ SMALL RED ONION, THINLY SLICED

1 POUND 2 OUNCES RIPE TOMATOES, PEELED AND CHOPPED

SALT

3 EGGS

FRESHLY GROUND BLACK PEPPER

DRIED OREGANO

This is something very simple that Greeks love to eat. Serve with some country-style bread, a dish of olives and a dish of feta.

Heat the oil in a large nonstick skillet over medium heat and sauté the onion until it begins to soften. Add the tomatoes and season with salt. Simmer for a few minutes to reduce, but leave some chunkiness. Break the eggs in, leave them for a bit until they start to set, then push them through the tomatoes with a wooden spoon until just cooked. Serve at once with a grind of pepper and a crumbling of oregano.

BAKER'S

FOODS

The yayia's (grandmother's) face in the bakery on the island of Lipsi broke into many more smiling creases as she saw the children. Her spontaneous arm stretched through the heavenly baker's air, past the spinach pies, cheese pies, all the other pies and the huge round pillows of breads until it landed on a sweet roll, which she broke in half for the children. The pure generosity and kindness that exists in so many of the older-faced generation who have eaten healthy food all their lives. And testimony to the fact that children in Greece are highly considered. There seems no problem about your child tearing around the avli (courtyard) of a restaurant with other children they have just found. No need to apologize or pretend that your children are normally far calmer than this.

PITA BREAD

Πίτα

MAKES 8

½ OUNCE FRESH YEAST,
OR 2 TEASPOONS ACTIVE
DRY YEAST

1 TEASPOON HONEY

3 CUPS BREAD FLOUR

6 TABLESPOONS OLIVE OIL

Generally in Greece pita is found at a souvlaki house (souvlatzithiko) and some grill places. But it is also wonderful served plain instead of bread at your table with dips.

In Greece, the pita are more often wrapped than stuffed for souvlaki and kebabs, so they need to be a bit softer. They are then heated up on the outdoor grill, or in the oven or griddle pan before filling. If you will be eating them right away, however, cook them a little longer, until they just start to color. These can be frozen once cooked and then just pulled out to thaw.

Crumble the fresh yeast or sprinkle the dried yeast into a large wide bowl, the same one that will hold your dough later

for rising. Add the honey and 3 tablespoons of warm water and mix to dissolve. Leave it till it starts to activate and get frothy. Add 1 heaped teaspoon of salt, the flour, oil and an extra 7 ounces of water to the dough and mix with a wooden spoon until a rough dough clumps around it. Change to your hands and knead until you have a soft springy dough, 8 to 10 minutes. It will seem sticky at first, but that is good, so only add more flour if the dough clings to your hands.

Wipe out the bowl with an oiled paper towel. Put the dough in, cover with plastic wrap, then a heavy cloth, and leave in a warm place until it has puffed up and almost doubled in size, 1½ to 2 hours.

Preheat the oven to 400°F. Punch the dough down and divide it into 8 balls about 3½ ounces each. Press each ball into a flat disk with your hands and leave for 5 minutes for them to relax.

Roll the disks out with a rolling pin to a circle of about 2½ inches in diameter and about ¹⁄₁₆ inch thick. Brush lightly with olive oil and put onto unfloured baking sheets. Bake one sheet at a time until they are firmed on the first side, 5 minutes or so, then turn them over and bake for another 3 minutes, or until the top surface is dry. You will finish cooking them under the broiler or in the oven when about to serve, so they should be a little underdone at this stage. Remove and immediately stack them on top of each other and wrap in plastic wrap to keep them limp so you will be able to wrap them around your kebabs. Alternatively, you can fry each bread in a hot dry skillet until just changed color but not browned, about 1 minute each side. Stack and wrap in plastic wrap as you go.

To serve, brush each side lightly with olive oil and put under the broiler to warm both sides, or use a hot griddle pan.

KOULOURIA SESAME BREAD RINGS

Κουλούρια

Koulouri means "coil" in Greece. I adore these for breakfast. Or with tarama or tirokafteri later on. They sometimes differ in size but generally are round, a bit flattened and slightly irregular in shape. These are sold on the streets by koulourades. The nice thing is that when you get them in a package, many sesame seeds fall to the bottom, then you can pour them out and eat them off your hand.

Crumble the fresh yeast or sprinkle the dried into a bowl. Add the sugar, 10½ ounces lukewarm water and a handful of flour. Whisk to smooth any lumps. Leave until it starts to activate and bubble, about 10 minutes. Add the rest of the flour, the salt and oil and mix with a wooden spoon until a loose dough forms. Knead on a lightly floured surface for 7 to 8 minutes or until the dough is smooth and spongy. Wipe out the bowl with an oiled paper towel and put the dough in.

Cover with plastic wrap, then a dish cloth, and leave in a warm spot for about 2 hours, until puffed and doubled in size.

Preheat the oven to 400°F and line 2 baking sheets with parchment paper. For the flour paste, mix the flour and water in a bowl until smooth. Knead the dough briefly, then divide it into 12 equal parts. Roll, stretch and coax each piece into a thin rope about 16 inches long. Make the first 6 and while baking, prepare the next batch. Brush each rope lightly with the paste, and sprinkle sesame seeds all over, then roll through the seeds that have dropped on your work surface so that they're covered all over. Turn each rope on itself, forming a ring, pressing the ends together to seal. Place on the baking sheets and bake for 20 minutes or until golden. Sesame seeds that have fallen onto the trays can be used elsewhere.

ELIOPSOMO OLIVE BREAD

Ελιόψωμο

MAKES 1 LOAF

½ OUNCE FRESH YEAST, OR
2 TEASPOONS ACTIVE DRY
YEAST

PINCH OF SUGAR

3 CUPS BREAD FLOUR

½ TEASPOON SALT

1 TABLESPOON OLIVE OIL,
PLUS EXTRA FOR BRUSHING

½ CUP DRAINED PITTED
KALAMATA OLIVES, HALVED

1 TEASPOON DRIED
OREGANO

SMALL SPRIG OF DRIED
OREGANO, FOR THE TOP

A myth narrates how Athina became the protectress of the city of Athens. At the moment of the foundation of the city, two gods offered to protect it, Poseidon and Athina. It was decided that the inhabitants would choose the god with the most useful and precious gift. Poseidon struck the ground with his trident and a horse was born. He said: "My gift is the horse, which will render you swifter and give you the strength to combat your enemies." (Another myth claims he created a well from which water shot forth but was salty, rendering it undrinkable.) Then it was Athina's turn. The goddess planted her staff into the ground and immediately it was transformed into a twisted tree with silver leaves, laden with small black fruits. The goddess said: "My gift is the olive tree; the juice of its fruits will bring peace, health and prosperity to you and your table." The inhabitants chose the gift of Athina. And dedicated the Parthenon to Athina as protectress of their city.

Most often olives in Greece are served just plain and are loved as they are. Apart from the generous handfuls that are tossed into salads, they are not used in cooking much.

Here is a lovely bread to use the wonderful Greek olives in. It's also good toasted.

Crumble the fresh or scatter the dried yeast into a large bowl. Add the sugar and 5½ ounces warm water and leave it to activate and bubble for about

10 minutes. Add the flour, salt and olive oil and mix first with a wooden spoon, then your hands to get a soft dough. Knead for 8 to 10 minutes, until smooth and spongy. Wipe out the bowl with a paper towel and put the dough in. Make a cross on the dough by pressing with the edge of your hand (to bless the dough). Cover the bowl with plastic wrap and then a dish cloth and put in a warm spot for a couple of hours to rise.

Pat the olives dry. Put them in a bowl with the oregano and toss well. When the dough has risen and is doubled in size, knead it again, this time working in the olives and oregano until they are evenly distributed.

You might need to use a little extra flour, as the olives will add some oil to the dough. Shape into an oval loaf, making sure a few olives are showing on the outside. Put on a baking sheet lined with parchment paper. Brush the bread with oil and if you have the sprig of oregano, press this onto the top. Cover with a dish cloth and leave in a warm spot for about 1 hour to rise again.

In the meantime, preheat the oven to 400°F. Bake the bread for about 30 minutes, until it is golden and sounds hollow when tapped on the base. Cool on a wire rack before slicing.

SPANAKOPITA SPINACH PIES

Σπανακόπιτα

MAKES 9

FILLING

5 TABLESPOONS OLIVE OIL

1½ CUPS CHOPPED GREEN
ONIONS WITH SOME GREEN

1 POUND 9 OUNCES
SPINACH LEAVES (ABOUT
2 BUNCHES), WASHED,
DRAINED AND SHREDDED

⅓ CUP COARSELY CHOPPED
FRESH DILL (INCLUDE SOME
STALKS)

SALT

7 OUNCES FETA, COARSELY
SHREDDED

2 EGGS, LIGHTLY BEATEN

FRESHLY GRATED NUTMEG

FRESHLY GROUND BLACK
PEPPER

27 SHEETS OF PHYLLO
PASTRY*, FINAL
DIMENSIONS 9 X 10 INCHES

OLIVE OIL, FOR BRUSHING

There are many variations on spinach pies in Greece involving different pastries and different fillings, some with feta and others just plain. This one has a little feta and uses phyllo pastry. These are delicious as a meal or snack.

You will need an oven dish of about 12¾ x 8 inches, as you will arrange them in a long row.

To make the filling, choose a nonstick pot that is large enough to take all the spinach. Add the oil and put over medium heat. Add the onions and sauté until softened. Add the spinach and a little salt, and cook, covered, until the spinach wilts, turning it through a couple of times. Flick in a little water if necessary, but there should be enough coming from the spinach. Now uncover and simmer until the spinach softens and most of the water has evaporated. Remove to a bowl to cool. Add the dill, feta, eggs, nutmeg and a few grinds of pepper. Mix thoroughly and taste a little for salt.

Preheat the oven to 350°F and grease a 12¾ x 8-inch baking dish. Cut your phyllo sheets and keep them covered with a dish cloth to prevent them from drying out. Now you will have to work quickly so that the pastry doesn't dry and crack, keeping the phyllo you are not working with covered with a dish cloth. Lay 1 phyllo sheet flat on a work surface and brush it well with olive oil. Lay another sheet neatly on top, brush it with oil and repeat once more, so that you have 3 layers. Now dollop 2 heaped tablespoons of filling along one short end, leaving a border of about an inch. Drag the filling into an even line, then

roll up the pastry fairly tightly
into a cigar shape starting from
the spinach end, making one
full turn, then turn and tuck the
sides over and continue rolling.
Brush the surface with oil. Make
8 more rolls in this way and
as they are finished, arrange
them in the dish side by side
so they all fit touching in a row
running from one short side to
the opposite side, like soldiers
all lined up. Bake for about 30
minutes or until golden. Cool a
dash before serving, as these are
best eaten warm.

* *The dimensions of commercial
phyllo vary from brand to brand,
so you will need to work out the
number of phyllo sheets you require
in the beginning, according to the
maker's dimensions.*

*The geography of Greece must have added
a lot to its specialness. So much coastline and
so much sea with thousands of islands. It looks
like a grand goddess was wading through the
waters in a flowing dress and she rested her
jewels down for a moment. Then time froze.
And there they are—her jewels—grown towns
with people in them. And she must be still
watching over them.*

TIROPITA CHEESE PIES

Τυρόπιτα

MAKES 9

FILLING

1 POUND FETA, COARSELY
SHREDDED

7 OUNCES RICOTTA

⅓ CUP MILK

27 SHEETS OF PHYLLO
PASTRY*, FINAL
DIMENSIONS 9 X 10 INCHES

OLIVE OIL, FOR BRUSHING

You can brush the pastry with melted butter rather than the olive oil if you prefer. Great if your phyllo sheets are 20 inches long on one side; then you can cut two out of one, and the waste is less. These are good served alone or with the spanakopita (page 168); then you can have one of each as a meal. Nice with a mixed salad.

To make the filling, put the feta, ricotta and milk in a bowl and mash together well.

Preheat the oven to 350°F and grease a 12¾ × 8-inch baking dish. Cut the phyllo sheets to size and keep them covered with a dish cloth to prevent them drying out. Now you will have to work quickly so that the pastry doesn't dry and crack, keeping the phyllo you are not working with covered with a dish cloth. Lay 1 phyllo sheet flat on a work surface and brush it all over with olive oil. Lay another sheet neatly on top, brush it with oil and repeat once more, so that you have 3 layers. Spoon 2 unheaped tablespoons of filling along one short end, leaving a border of about an inch. Drag the filling into an even line from one side to the other, then roll it up in the pastry fairly tightly, making one complete turn to cover the feta, then tucking the sides in and continuing to roll.

Brush the surface with oil. Make 8 more rolls in this way and arrange them in the dish side by side so they all fit in a row running from one short side to the opposite side, keeping seam sides up so that leaks can stay on top.

Bake for about 30 minutes or until golden. Cool a little before serving, as these are best eaten warm.

* *The dimensions of commercial phyllo vary from brand to brand, so you will need to work out the number of phyllo sheets you require in the beginning, according to the maker's dimensions.*

TIROPITA ME ANITHO CHEESE PIE WITH DILL

Τυρόπιτα με άνιθο

SERVES MANY

1 CUP ALL-PURPOSE FLOUR, PLUS EXTRA FOR ROLLING

¼ TEASPOON BAKING POWDER

1 TABLESPOON OLIVE OIL

¼–½ CUP WARM WATER

FILLING

9 OUNCES FETA

9 OUNCES ANTHOTIRO CHEESE OR SOFT RICOTTA

1 TABLESPOON MILK

1 TABLESPOON OLIVE OIL

2 HEAPING TABLESPOONS COARSELY CHOPPED DILL

FRESHLY GROUND BLACK PEPPER

2 EGGS

This is a flat, salty feta pie with dill that Roulla, a lovely lady in Mani, taught me. She used one of those great colored plastic bowls that you would do your hand washing in to mix her cheese, as she was making three times this amount for family and friends.

There is no salt in the pastry here because of the filling, so if you will be using the pastry for other purposes you can add a dash.

The dowel rod that many Greek housewives use as a rolling pin is very long and very thin, and they are able to roll out their pastry paper-thin by wrapping it around this rod and rolling it together.

Preheat the oven to 325°F and grease the base of a 12-inch pie dish or pan. Put the flour and baking powder into a bowl. Add the olive oil and mix, then start adding the water, enough to make a lovely soft dough. Knead until smooth, about a minute. Cover with plastic wrap and leave at room temperature for 20 minutes or so.

For the filling, coarsely shred the feta into a large bowl. Shred the anthotiro also, if using, and add to the bowl; otherwise just add the ricotta. Mash it all together well. Add the milk, olive oil, dill and a good grind of pepper. Lightly whisk the eggs in a small bowl and pour all but a tablespoon in with the cheeses. Mix until well combined; if it seems stiff, thin it out with a little milk just to loosen up the mixture a bit, then cover and set aside while you roll the dough.

Roll out the dough to a $\frac{1}{16}$-inch-thick circle about 16 inches in diameter. Drape it over your rolling pin or dowel rod, then lower it into the pie dish, leaving the overhang for now. Scrape the filling mix on top and spread it evenly. Turn the pastry overhangs over the cheese mix so that you leave an uncovered area of about 2 inches in the middle. The pastry will be doubled over in places in an irregular way and that's how it is, but you can cut away a little where it's too thick. Brush the pastry with the remaining egg.

Bake in the oven until the bottom of the pastry is firm and the top is golden, about 40 minutes. Remove and cool a bit before cutting into thin slices. Good served warm or at room temperature.

HORTOPITA WILD GREENS PIE

Χορτόπιτα

MAKES ABOUT 35; SERVES A COUPLE OF CLASSES

PASTRY

4 CUPS ALL-PURPOSE FLOUR

1 TEASPOON BAKING POWDER

SALT

¼ CUP OLIVE OIL

1⅓ CUPS COLD WATER

FILLING

1 POUND 9 OUNCES LEAVES OF MIXED WILD GREENS (SUCH AS BELGIAN ENDIVE, MUSTARD GREENS OR TURNIP GREENS), INCLUDING SOME SPINACH

3½ OUNCES GREEN ONIONS, CHOPPED

½ CUP CHOPPED DILL

½ CUP CHOPPED ITALIAN PARSLEY

¼ CUP CHOPPED FENNEL FRONDS

10½ OUNCES FETA, CRUMBLED

SALT AND FRESHLY GROUND BLACK PEPPER

OLIVE OIL, FOR BRUSHING

This is from the principal of the elementary school Hill, in Plaka Athens. Every year he makes it together with students and it is then distributed to the school. He says to make this, one needs "meraki" (presence and heart, fun and patience). One should not consider the fact that the kitchen may be a mess afterward on account of all the greens and flour everywhere. The pita, he says, is a success if, when you cut it, it is dry, not oily or damp. Then you know you have done well. And this pita furthermore needs special music to succeed–klarino (clarinet), defi (frame drum), violi (violin) and laouto (lute), the classic Epirus band instruments. Only these, nothing else.

The original recipe is 7 layers of thinly rolled pastry, handfuls of wild poppy grass, stinging nettles, sorrel and 2 bunches of dill, and 3 handfuls of flour and various wild mountain grasses and leaves. You may mix in whatever of these you can find into the amount of greens given here. The wilder they are, the more wonderful the flavor.

To make the pastry, put the flour and baking powder in a bowl with a big pinch of salt. Add the olive oil and stir in enough of the water to give a rough dough that clumps around your spoon. Now use your hands and knead the dough until smooth. Divide into 7 balls of about 4¾ ounces each and leave them to rest at room temperature while you make the filling.

For the filling, rinse the mixed leaves and drain in a colander. Chop coarsely and put in a big bowl. Add the green onions, dill, parsley, fennel and feta, and season with a good amount of pepper and some salt (even though there is feta here, it will still need about a teaspoon). Mix very well.

Preheat the oven to 350°F and brush the base and sides of a 14¼-inch round baking pan with olive oil. On a floured surface, roll out one of the pastry balls to the diameter of your baking tin. Because the pastry is so stretchy, you'll be able to pull it to fit, so just hold the pan over the rolled pastry to check that it's about the right size. Drape it over your rolling pin and lower it into the tin, stretching it if necessary to fit. Brush lightly with olive oil. Roll out another ball of pastry to cover the first. Brush with olive oil. Only the bottom of the pie will have a double layer of pastry.

Divide the filling into roughly 5 parts, then scatter one-fifth over the pastry base. Roll out another pastry ball, and now it is more manageable to brush it with olive oil before putting it over the greens. Scatter with another one-fifth of the greens and continue layering one sheet of oiled pastry then a fifth of the greens, finishing with a final pastry layer, making sure that it completely covers the greens. Neaten the edges by crimping the pastry or simply pushing any excess down the sides of the pan. Brush with olive oil. Bake for 1 to 1¼ hours, until the top is crisp and golden.

Cool slightly before cutting into diamonds and serving.

CHANIOTIKO BOUREKI VEGETABLE PIE FROM CHANIA

Χανιώτικο μπουρέκι

SERVES 12

10½ OUNCES POTATOES, CUT INTO ⅛ INCH-THICK SLICES

1 POUND 10 OUNCES ZUCCHINI, CUT INTO ⅛-INCH-THICK SLICES

2 TABLESPOONS CHOPPED MINT

2 TABLESPOONS CHOPPED ITALIAN PARSLEY

1 POUND 2 OUNCES SOFT MIZITHRA CHEESE OR RICOTTA

½ CUP SHREDDED KEFALOTIRI CHEESE OR PARMESAN

1 EGG, LIGHTLY BEATEN

½ CUP OLIVE OIL

½ CUP MILK

⅔ CUP ALL-PURPOSE FLOUR

LARGE PINCH OF GRATED NUTMEG

SALT AND FRESHLY GROUND BLACK PEPPER

1 LARGE RIPE TOMATO, PEELED AND COARSELY CHOPPED

A friend of mine, Nikos, from Chania in northern Crete, taught me this. If you can't find soft mizithra cheese, you can use ricotta. Lovely layers of vegetables are first baked and then a pastry layer is added on and the pie is finished in the oven.

Preheat the oven to 350°F. Put the vegetables, herbs, cheeses, the beaten egg, olive oil, milk, flour and nutmeg into a bowl. Add salt and a little pepper. Mix well with your hands, massaging it all together. Spread roughly three-quarters of the mix over the bottom of an 8½ × 12-inch baking dish. Scatter the chopped tomato over this, then add the rest of the mix. Smooth the surface and poke holes through the mixture here and there with the end of a wooden spoon. Pour about ½ cup of water into the emptied mixture bowl, swirl to rinse it, then pour the water over the mixture in the dish, rocking it to distribute the water. Bake for about 45 minutes, or until the vegetables are tender.

Meanwhile, make the pastry. Sift the flour and salt into a bowl. Mix in the olive oil and enough of the water to give a rough dough that clumps together. Knead until firm. Cover with plastic wrap and set aside at room temperature.

Take the dish from the oven (leaving the oven on) when the vegetables are ready and set aside to cool a little.

Roll the dough out on a

lightly floured surface to a
rectangle slightly bigger than
the dish size. It will be very thin,
just $\frac{1}{16}$ inch. Let rest for a couple
of minutes, then fit it over the
pie. Push down the edges with
a knife so that it curves down
the sides, or just fold the pastry
over to give a neat border. Brush
the surface with egg. Gently cut
through just the pastry into 12
portions. Sprinkle the top with
the sesame seeds and return to
the oven for about 20 minutes
until the pastry is crisp and
golden. Cut into the premarked
portions and serve warm.

PASTRY

$\frac{2}{3}$ CUP ALL-PURPOSE
FLOUR

$\frac{1}{2}$ TEASPOON SALT

1 TABLESPOON OLIVE OIL

$\frac{1}{2}$ CUP WATER

1 EGG, LIGHTLY BEATEN,
FOR BRUSHING

1 HEAPING TEASPOON
SESAME SEEDS

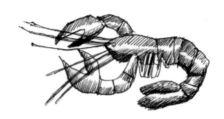

SOUPS

Hurtling through the villages, along old, curled streets that cars these days can only just about get through. Past thick white walls that look like feta into places where time stops. Men go out for coffee and tavli (backgammon). Women are at home preparing food. Times gone from many places. And yet–a simplicity that many parts of Greece still tell us of.

KAKAVIA FISHERMAN'S SOUP

Κακαβιά

This is the type of chunky soup that a fisherman would make on his boat. Often the fish are left whole, but here I have first made a broth, strained it and then cooked fillets of fish in it to avoid bones swimming around. It is so simple. Potatoes, onions, garlic, chunks of tomato and fish.

Make a broth. Put the soup fish into a stock pot and cover with 4 cups of cold water. Add the bunch of parsley, piece of celery, whole garlic clove, salt and a couple of grinds of pepper. Peel the onion and cut off a piece from one side. Add this piece to the stock pot. Chop what's left of the onion and put to one side for the moment. Bring the pot to a boil. Lower the heat and simmer for about 20 minutes. Strain, discarding parsley, celery and the bones and skin of the fish. Depending on the fish you've used, you may be able to salvage some flesh for another use. You should have about 3 cups of broth.

Heat the oil in a large wide pot over medium heat and sauté the chopped onion until softened and pale golden. Add the chopped celery and sauté until that softens too. Next add the chopped garlic and cook until you can smell it, then add the wine. Cook until the wine has almost evaporated, then add the tomatoes, potatoes, some salt and pepper and simmer for about 5 minutes. Add the fish broth and simmer for another 5 minutes before adding the fillets. Lower the heat and simmer uncovered until it loses the watery look and the fish is cooked through, 10 minutes or so. Add the lemon juice and the chopped parsley, rock the pot to distribute it all gently and taste for salt. Add a grind of pepper and serve hot with bread.

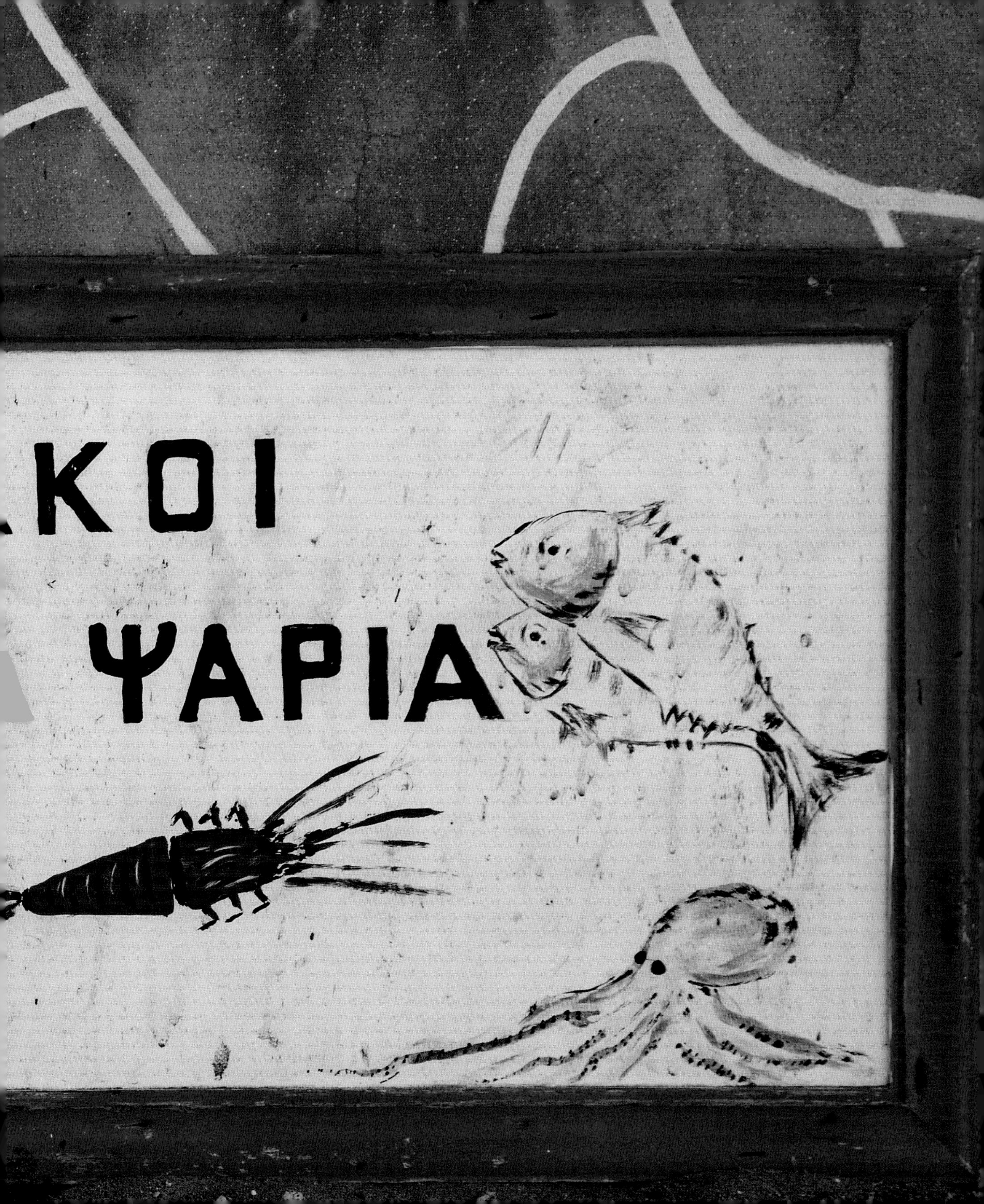
ΚΟΙ
ΨΑΡΙΑ

PSAROSOUPA AVGOLEMONO EGG + LEMON FISH SOUP

Ψαρόσουπα αυγολέμονο

SERVES 4

2¼ POUNDS WHOLE FISH
(SUCH AS SEA BASS, BREAM
OR SNAPPER), SCALED AND
CLEANED

1 CELERY RIB WITH LEAVES

1 SMALL ONION, PEELED

1 GARLIC CLOVE, PEELED

1 SMALL HANDFUL ITALIAN
PARSLEY WITH STALKS

SALT AND FRESHLY GROUND
BLACK PEPPER

⅔ CUP MEDIUM-GRAIN RICE

JUICE OF 2 LEMONS

2 EGGS

BEST OLIVE OIL, FOR
SERVING

This is probably the most well-known of Greek soups. It is often made with chicken and sometimes even lamb. Here, the boiled fish is lovely served after the soup, with a drizzle of olive oil or a dish of skordalia (a small scattering of cinnamon over the soup is also lovely).

Cut the head and tail off the fish but don't discard them. Put the celery, onion, garlic, parsley and 10 cups of water in a large wide pot. Season with salt and pepper and bring to a boil. Add the fish body, head and tail. Simmer, uncovered, for 20 to 30 minutes, depending on the thickness of the fish. Skim off any scum that may settle on the surface. Remove from the heat. Discard the head and tail and gently take out the fish. Take off the skin and carefully remove the natural long fillets, discarding the spine and bones. Put the fillets on a plate, cover and keep warm. Discard the celery, onion, garlic and parsley and strain the broth into a clean pot. You should have about 6 cups. Add the rice and simmer for about 20 minutes, or until tender.

Whisk the lemon juice and eggs with a little salt in a bowl. Add a ladleful of hot broth to acclimatize the egg, then slowly stir the mixture into the broth. Immediately remove from the heat and stir long enough for the egg to just cook through but not form scrambled bits. Taste for salt.

Ladle the soup into bowls and grind a little pepper on top. Serve the fish after or next to the soup, with a drizzle of olive oil.

PSARI VRASTO LADOLEMONO POACHED FISH WITH LEMON OIL

Ψάρι βραστό (λαδολέμονο)

SERVES 3

1 LARGE POTATO, PEELED, HALVED AND CUT INTO 5 OR 6 PIECES

2 CARROTS, CUT INTO 1¼-INCH ROUNDS

2 ZUCCHINI, CUT INTO ¾–1¼-INCH ROUNDS

1 SMALL CELERY RIB WITH LEAVES (ABOUT 2¼ OUNCES), OR SMALL BUNCH OF GREEK-STYLE CELERY

ABOUT 1½ OUNCES GREEN ONIONS, WHITE PART ONLY

SALT

1 FIRM BONELESS WHITE FISH FILLET, SUCH AS OCEAN PERCH OR LING (ABOUT 15½ OUNCES)

LEMON OIL

JUICE OF 1 LARGE JUICY LEMON

¼ CUP BEST-QUALITY EXTRA VIRGIN OLIVE OIL

SALT

1 TABLESPOON COARSELY CHOPPED ITALIAN PARSLEY

FRESHLY GROUND BLACK PEPPER

I love this. It's delicate yet aromatic, not quite a soup. It is an easy, healthy, almost instant food that you could serve to any generation. You will need a nice big and wide pot here, as there is not too much liquid and the ingredients all need to float comfortably. You can use any firm white fish fillets that won't break up too much.

Greek celery is amazing and seems to give a wonderful flavor to their soups. It has lovely clumps and small thin ribs and leaves that look almost like parsley—you might never guess that it's celery if you found it at the market.

Put the potato, carrot, zucchini, celery and onions into a wide pot and add 3 cups of water. Season with salt. Bring to a boil and simmer uncovered for about 15 minutes. Add the fish, shuffling the vegetables if necessary to ensure that the fish is covered by the broth. Simmer, uncovered, over low heat for 10 to 15 minutes (depending on the thickness of the fish), until the fish is cooked through but not breaking up.

For the lemon oil, whip the lemon juice and oil with a little salt in a bowl until thick and creamy.

Remove the soup from the heat and discard the onion and celery. Pour in the lemon oil and rock the pot to distribute it well. Leave it for a few minutes so the flavors mingle, and check your seasoning. Scatter in the parsley. Remove the fish to a bowl and break it up into 3 pieces using a fork and spoon. To serve, put 1 piece of fish per bowl, a couple of pieces of each vegetable, a good ladleful of broth and a grind of pepper.

TRAHANA SOUP

Τραχανάς

SERVES 6

7 OUNCES TRAHANA

1 BOUILLON CUBE (NO MSG, FROM HEALTH FOOD STORES), OR 2 CUPS HOMEMADE VEGETABLE BROTH

ABOUT 1½ CUPS MILK

7 OUNCES FETA, CUT INTO LARGE BLOCKS

OLIVE OIL, FOR SERVING

FRESHLY GROUND BLACK PEPPER

LEMON QUARTERS, FOR SERVING

Trahana is bulgur wheat dried with yogurt, popular in villages and mountains. It is available from Greek food stores. There are two types: sweet and sour. I love the sour one.

Trahana is wonderful. I have loved it since I was small, but I know friends who used to come to us were a bit surprised by it. It may take some getting used to, but it feels like one of those soups you would imagine from a Russian fairy tale. When cooked it becomes like a creamy thin savory oatmeal. Perfect for a cold winter night. Chunks of feta are added at the end and heated to just surrender stage. The soup is served with a drizzle of olive oil and those who want can squeeze some lemon in, even though the soup itself is a bit on the sour side.

Keep any uncooked trahana in a sealed bag in the fridge.

Put the trahana into a wide pot. Cover with 4 cups of hot water, put the lid on and leave for about 3 hours. Add the bouillon cube with another 2 cups of hot water (or homemade broth), bring to a boil, then simmer, uncovered, for about 45 minutes, stirring often so the trahana doesn't stick to the bottom. Halfway through, add the milk and 1 cup of water. You want it thick but spoonable, so add extra water if necessary to thin it; you could need quite a bit more or none, depending on your trahana. It should melt to a creamy thin porridge, but if it is very chunky to start with, you might have to pulse with a hand-held blender to get rid of any chunky bits. Add the feta in the last few minutes, just long enough to soften but keep the pieces whole. Serve in bowls with a splash of olive oil, some pepper and a squeeze of lemon.

FASOLADA WHITE BEAN SOUP
Φασολάδα

SERVES 6

1 POUND 2 OUNCES DRIED BUTTER (OR CANNELLINI, HARICOT, NAVY) BEANS

3 GARLIC CLOVES, 1 WHOLE, 2 CHOPPED

1 BAY LEAF

1 SMALL CELERY RIB

½ SMALL ONION

SALT

¼ CUP OLIVE OIL

1 LARGE ONION, CHOPPED

3 CARROTS, PEELED, CUT INTO NICE CHUNKS

14-OUNCE CAN CHOPPED TOMATOES

FRESHLY GROUND BLACK PEPPER

1¾ OUNCES RED OR GREEN ONIONS, COARSELY CHOPPED

½ CUP VERY COARSELY CHOPPED ITALIAN PARSLEY

¼ CUP COARSELY CHOPPED CELERY LEAVES

BEST-QUALITY OLIVE OIL, FOR SERVING

This is a wonderful wintry chunky soup. My friend Lisa brought this version to our table one Sunday for lunch, and I loved it. Depending on the beans you use, you may need to add more water. Often smaller beans are used, but this is also lovely with the bigger butter beans. This was originally a poor man's dish. Cheap and filling but beloved and comforting, and people would often exclaim, "If only we had a fasolada now!" Use best-quality olive oil.

Cover the beans with plenty of cold water and soak overnight. The next day, drain and rinse them, and put into a pot with cold water to cover. Bring to a boil, skimming off any scum that has formed. Drain and rinse again. Wipe any scum that has collected on the pot, then return the beans to it. Add 8 cups of cold water, the whole garlic clove, bay leaf, celery rib and the ½ onion. Simmer, partly covered, for about an hour, until tender. Larger beans will take longer and will need more water. Add salt in the last 10 minutes or so.

Meanwhile, heat the oil in a soup pot over medium heat and sauté the chopped onion until soft and golden. Add the chopped garlic and carrots and when the garlic smells good, add the tomatoes. Season with salt and pepper. Swish about ½ cup of water in the tomato can and pour into the pot. Put the lid on and simmer for 10 minutes or so. When the beans are ready, pour them and their water in with the tomato sauce. Simmer for 10 minutes, adding a little water if it's too thick. Ladle into bowls and serve with red onion, parsley and celery leaves on top, a drizzle of oil and a grinding of pepper.

FAKES LENTIL SOUP

Φακές

SERVES 5 OR 6

6 TABLESPOONS RED WINE VINEGAR

4 GARLIC CLOVES, PEELED

1 DRIED OREGANO SPRIG, OR 1 FRESH ROSEMARY SPRIG

2 BAY LEAVES

1½ CUPS SMALL BROWN LENTILS

6 TABLESPOONS OLIVE OIL

1 LARGE ONION, FINELY CHOPPED

1 CARROT, PEELED AND CUT INTO CHUNKS

1 CINNAMON STICK

10½ OUNCES RIPE TOMATOES, COARSELY GRATED (SO THE SKIN STAYS BEHIND IN YOUR HAND)

SALT AND FRESHLY GROUND BLACK PEPPER

BEST-QUALITY OLIVE OIL, FOR SERVING

This is a soup that most Greeks have grown up with. The unusual part of this healthy, nourishing soup is the way they serve it with a drizzle of vinegar. They say that the vitamins in carrots help us absorb the iron in lentils better and so they should be cooked together.

Put the vinegar into a bowl. Crush 1 of the garlic cloves and add it to the bowl along with the oregano or rosemary sprig and 1 of the bay leaves.

Rinse the lentils, then put them into a pot with 7 cups of cold water. Add the remaining garlic cloves and bay leaf, the olive oil, onion, carrot and cinnamon stick and bring to a boil. Skim the surface if necessary, cover and simmer gently for about 25 minutes. Add the tomatoes, season well with salt and a little pepper and simmer for 20 minutes, or until the lentils are soft and the soup is lovely and thick. Take the lid off and simmer for about 5 minutes or longer if necessary, until it has a lovely thick soupy consistency. Take off the heat, splash in 3 tablespoons of the vinegar and leave it to stand for a few minutes before serving.

Serve hot, with an extra drizzle of olive oil and with the remaining vinegar on the table for anyone who'd like more.

LADERA

+ SALADS

The smell of a Greek manavi (greengrocer) . . . especially old-style ones or on the islands re-blossoms each time I walk into one. It is a warm, extremely friendly and comforting smell . . . like flowers, leaves, melons, figs, meadows, orchards, the sea and sweet life all rolled into one store.

REVITHADA BAKED CHICKPEAS

Ρεβυθάδα

SERVES MANY

1 POUND 2 OUNCES DRIED CHICKPEAS

1 TABLESPOON ALL-PURPOSE FLOUR

2 ONIONS, WELL CHOPPED

2 BAY LEAVES

6 TABLESPOONS OLIVE OIL

SALT AND FRESHLY GROUND BLACK PEPPER

BEST-QUALITY OLIVE OIL, FOR SERVING

LEMON QUARTERS, FOR SERVING, OPTIONAL

The traditional Sunday lunch in Sifnos is chickpeas. The skepastaria, or special ceramic pot, which is often passed down from mother to daughter, is taken on Saturday afternoon to the baker to cook overnight in the wood oven. Then everyone collects theirs on Sunday morning.

Here the chickpeas are cooked for quite a while in a regular oven.

If you have a ceramic pot about 9 inches in diameter with a lid, great. If not, a baking or gratin dish with a lid will work well. It really is the pot, good olive oil and maybe the wonderful surrounds of a Greek island that can make a dish special.

Put the chickpeas and flour in a bowl, cover with plenty of cold water and soak overnight. Preheat the oven to 400°F. Drain the chickpeas, rinse and put into a large round ceramic pot with a good-fitting lid. Cover with 4 cups of water and add the onions, bay leaves and olive oil. Stir a few times to distribute the onion, then put the lid on. Bake in the oven for 2 hours.

Lower the temperature to 350°F and remove the pot from the oven. The contents should be nice and bubbly. Season well with salt and pepper and mix. Return the pot, still covered, to the oven for a further 2 hours, when the chickpeas will be lovely and soft with a little of the thick liquid left. Turn off the oven and leave the covered pot inside to cool for about 1 hour. Taste for salt and pepper, then serve warm, with a drizzle of olive oil and a squeeze of lemon juice, if you like.

YIGANDES BAKED GIANT BUTTER BEANS

Γίγαντες

SERVES 6 TO 8

1 POUND 2 OUNCES DRIED GIANT BUTTER (FAVA) BEANS

1 BAY LEAF

4 GARLIC CLOVES, 2 WHOLE, 2 CHOPPED

SALT

½ CUP OLIVE OIL

1 LARGE RED ONION, CHOPPED

14-OUNCE CAN CRUSHED TOMATOES

1 TABLESPOON TOMATO PASTE

FRESHLY GROUND BLACK PEPPER

2 HEAPING TABLESPOONS COARSELY CHOPPED ITALIAN PARSLEY

4 THYME SPRIGS

In Greece, a lot of legumes are eaten as a main meal, and their long-cooked beans are especially wonderful. If you can't get the giant beans, then cannellini or other small beans will do. The beans will need soaking overnight. I use a ceramic round dish about 9 inches in diameter with a lid.

Put the beans in a bowl with plenty of cold water and soak overnight. Drain and rinse, then put into a pot and cover well with water. Bring to a boil, skimming off any scum that comes to the surface. Drain and give the beans a shower in a colander. Wipe off any scum from the sides of the pot. Return the beans to the pot, cover with plenty of water and add the bay leaf and 2 whole garlic cloves. Bring to a boil, lower the heat and cook, partly covered, for about 1¼ hours, until the beans are tender. Skim the surface when necessary. Add salt just toward the end. Preheat the oven to 350°F.

Meanwhile, heat the oil in a heatproof casserole dish and sauté the onion until golden. Add the chopped garlic and cook until it smells good, then add the tomatoes and tomato paste and some salt and pepper. Swish the tomato can with a few tablespoons of water and add to the tomato. Simmer uncovered for a few minutes. Add the parsley and thyme sprigs. Remove from the heat.

When the beans are tender, transfer with a slotted spoon to the casserole. Add enough of the bean cooking water to just cover. Mix gently. Taste for salt and pepper. Cover and bake for 45 minutes, or until beans are creamy and there is some thickened sauce left in the pot. Take the lid off and bake until a bit crusty on top, 15 minutes or so. Cool a little before serving.

ΜΠΙΣΚΟΤΑ

♛

Ρούλια

ΜΠΙΣΚΟΤΑ · Αφοι Γ. ΡΟΥΛΙΑ
ΑΘΗΝΑΙ · ΕΛΛΑΣ

ΒΙΟΜΗΧΑΝΙΑ ΜΠΙΣΚΟΤΩΝ

FASOLAKIA YACHNI STEWED GREEN BEANS IN TOMATO

Φασολάκια γιαχνί

SERVES ABOUT 6

1¾ POUND ITALIAN FLAT BEANS (ROMANO BEANS)

5 TABLESPOONS OLIVE OIL

1 RED ONION, CHOPPED

3 GARLIC CLOVES, CHOPPED

14-OUNCE CAN CRUSHED TOMATOES

2 TABLESPOONS COARSELY CHOPPED ITALIAN PARSLEY

SALT AND FRESHLY GROUND BLACK PEPPER

¼ TEASPOON GROUND CINNAMON

This is often served as an entrée in Greece, with feta to mingle in with the sauce, and bread. Of course it's also great served next to an entrée such as roast meat or fish.

I have also seen potatoes added to the stew.

Cut the tops off the beans and string them if necessary. Rinse and drain, keeping them in your colander for now.

Heat the olive oil in a large nonstick pot over medium heat and sauté the onion until softened and almost sticky. Add the garlic and, when you can smell it, add the tomatoes, parsley, 2 or 3 grinds of pepper and a good amount of salt.

Simmer, uncovered, over medium heat for about 8 minutes, until the tomatoes soften and collapse.

Add the beans and 1 cup of hot water. Scatter the cinnamon over the beans and put the lid on. When it comes to a boil, turn the beans through, then put the lid back on and simmer until the beans are soft, about 20 minutes, mixing a few times so that no lonely beans sit out of the sauce for long. At the end of this time there should be a good amount of thickish sauce. If you think it needs it, stir in a little water. Turn off the heat and leave them for a while, covered, to absorb the flavors. Take the pot to the table and serve warm.

BAMIES
BAKED OKRA

Μπάμιες

SERVES ABOUT 8

1 POUND 5 OUNCES SMALL OKRA

⅓ CUP WINE VINEGAR

1 TABLESPOON COARSE SALT

6 TABLESPOONS OLIVE OIL

1 LARGE RED ONION, CHOPPED

2 SMALL GREEN SWEET PEPPERS (ABOUT 2¼ OUNCES EACH), HALVED LENGTHWISE, SEEDED AND SLICED

2 GARLIC CLOVES, FINELY CHOPPED

14-OUNCE CAN CHOPPED TOMATOES

2 TABLESPOONS CHOPPED ITALIAN PARSLEY

FRESHLY GROUND BLACK PEPPER

Okra is enjoyed in Greece when in season. It is often stewed on the stove but here is baked, which I really like. Also called ladies' fingers, it is rather a particular vegetable, containing a glutinous substance that thickens dishes. It is great served with a dish of feta and some bread and perhaps a green salad. Try and get small okra, about 1½ inches in length, so there is less chance of tough or stringy ones. This dish is sometimes also baked with chicken pieces in it.

Rinse and drain the okra. Trim the top of their hard stems in a circular conical way so that the top isn't pierced and no seeds can leak out. Put them into a bowl of cold water with the vinegar and salt and leave for an hour or so. Drain into a colander and rinse well.

Preheat the oven to 350°F. Heat the olive oil in a nonstick skillet over medium heat and sauté the onion until soft and sticky. Add the peppers toward the end, sauté for a couple of minutes, then add the garlic. When you can smell it frying, add the tomatoes. Simmer for about 5 minutes, smoothing any tomato lumps with a wooden spoon. Stir in 2 cups of water and the parsley, and season with salt and pepper. Add the okra, gently turning them to coat well.

Transfer to an 8½ × 12-inch baking dish or pan and bake uncovered for about 50 minutes. Gently turn the okra over and continue baking until the okra are roasted looking and the sauce is thick and dark and no longer watery, about 30 minutes. If it seems like the okra are getting too dark too quickly, turn the oven down slightly. Taste one to see if it is lovely and soft. Cool a little before serving to allow the okra to absorb the juices.

BRIAM MIXED ROAST VEGETABLES

Μπριάμ

2 SMALL EGGPLANTS
(1 POUND 5 OUNCES
TOTAL)

2–3 ZUCCHINI (10½ OUNCES
TOTAL), CUT INTO ⅝-INCH-
THICK SLICES

5–6 TOMATOES (1¾ POUND
TOTAL), HALF GRATED,
HALF CUT INTO CHUNKS

10½ OUNCES POTATOES,
CUT INTO ½-INCH-THICK
SLICES

1 LARGE RED ONION,
CUT INTO THIN RINGS

ABOUT 5 SMALL RED
PEPPERS OR 1 LARGE RED
BELL PEPPER, CUT INTO
THICK STRIPS

½ CUP OLIVE OIL

SALT AND FRESHLY
GROUND BLACK PEPPER

1 TEASPOON DRIED
OREGANO

It's wonderful to have a huge dish of mixed roasted vegetables that can be a meal on its own or can stand next to almost anything. This is nice warm or at room temperature. It will need quite a while in the oven for a lovely chunky result. You can also add other vegetables of your choice.

Quarter the eggplants lengthwise, then cut into ½-inch slices. Put them in a colander, sprinkle with salt and leave to drain away their juices for about 30 minutes. Wipe dry with paper towels. Preheat the oven to 350°F. Put all the vegetables into a 13-inch or so round, or of similar dimension, baking dish and drizzle the oil over. Add salt and pepper, and crumble the oregano over the top with your fingers. Cover tightly with aluminum foil and bake for about 2 hours or until all the vegetables are tender. Remove the foil and roast for 40 minutes or so more, until the vegetables are lovely and roasted and the sauce is reduced and a bit sticky. Taste for salt.

HORTA WILD GREENS

Χόρτα

SERVES 4 TO 6

ABOUT 2¼ POUNDS
WILD GREENS

BEST-QUALITY OLIVE OIL,
FOR SERVING

RED WINE VINEGAR,
FOR SERVING

LEMON QUARTERS,
FOR SERVING

You will find wild greens everywhere in Greece. It's a great idea to order them out—most tavernas seem to have them—and if you have them at the start of your meal, you will have this healthy dish going while you wait for the rest. When you buy them at the market for cooking, you will need an industrial amount even for just one family but even so, it is well worth it. Some are slightly bitter but are very healthy. There are some sweeter varieties called vlita, also grabbed in armfuls from the mountainsides and fields. Use any wild greens that you can find when making them at home or a mixture of a few different ones, such as belgian endive, dandelion and mustard leaves, and root vegetable tops such as turnip and beet can also be mixed in. You can add a few ladlefuls of the cooking water to a soup or boil some pasta and rice in it, or just drink some of the cooking water with a squeeze of lemon in it. Delicious and healthful.

To prepare the greens, snap off and discard any thick stalks; otherwise keep the whole leaf if it is young. Rinse them in cold water and shake dry. Bring a large pot of salted water to a boil and add the leaves, pushing them down and turning them over with tongs until they have all wilted. Simmer until the leaves are tender but not soggy and until the stems are no longer crisp—the cooking time will depend on your greens. Drain well.

To serve, drizzle with olive oil and splash over a little vinegar. Serve some lemon on the side.

ANGINARES ME KOUKIA ARTICHOKES + FAVA BEANS

Αγγινάρες με κουκιά

SERVES 8

3 POUNDS 5 OUNCES FAVA BEANS IN THEIR PODS (9 OUNCES SHELLED AND SKINNED)

JUICE OF 2½ LEMONS

8 ARTICHOKES (7¾ OUNCES EACH) WITH A STEM OF ABOUT 2½ INCHES

½ CUP OLIVE OIL

3 LARGE GREEN ONIONS, TRIMMED AND COARSELY CHOPPED

SALT AND FRESHLY GROUND BLACK PEPPER

2 TABLESPOONS CHOPPED DILL

1 TABLESPOON COARSELY CHOPPED MINT

This is a beautiful spring dish. It can be served as a side dish or as an entrée with a plate of feta and some bread. Fresh peas are also lovely here if you prefer them to the fava beans. Drizzle a little extra olive oil over to serve, and pepper.

Shell the beans and take off their outer jackets (if they don't come off easily you can drop them in boiling water for a few seconds). The small very green beans can be left, as their jackets are not tough. Put the juice of 1½ lemons in a large nonreactive bowl of cold water. Snap the tough outer leaves off the artichokes and discard. You may need to remove more than you think before you get to the tender leaves. Slice off the hard top of the leaves, maybe even one-third of the top depending on the size and type of artichoke. Leave 1½ inches or so of stalk and cut off the rest. Using a potato peeler or small sharp knife, peel the stems and the base of the artichokes. Halve them from top to bottom, then remove the choke with a small knife or pointed spoon. Put the cleaned artichokes immediately into the lemon water to prevent them from darkening.

Heat the oil in a large nonstick skillet over medium heat. Add the onions and gently sauté until pale gold.

Drain the artichokes, pat dry with paper towels and add them to the skillet in a single layer. Cook, turning once, until slightly colored. Season with salt and pepper, add 1 cup of water, put the lid on and simmer for 10 minutes, or until just tender and there is a little thickened sauce left in the skillet. If there isn't much sauce left, add a little hot water. Add the fava beans, leave the lid off and cook for another few minutes. Sprinkle in the remaining lemon juice, dill and mint, rocking the skillet so everything can mingle. Remove from the heat and leave for a few minutes before serving. This can also be served at room temperature but is best warm.

The same ingredients are lovely served raw with best olive oil, a piece of cheese and bread, pita or koulouria. Simply shelled fava beans, cleaned artichokes, green onions, fresh dill and mint leaves. Serve with ouzo on ice.

EHI TIS ORES TOU —IT HAS ITS MOMENTS

said the barman while I was waiting for a freshly squeezed orange juice and the juicer wasn't working. There was a lovely acceptance in this . . .

PANTZAROSALATA BEETS WITH YOGURT + PISTACHIOS

Παντζαροσαλάτα

SERVES 4 TO 6

1 POUND 7 OUNCES BEETS (ABOUT 4), LEAVES TRIMMED, OR 1 POUND 2 OUNCES CANNED BEETS

3 TABLESPOONS OLIVE OIL

JUICE OF ½ LEMON

2 GARLIC CLOVES, FINELY CHOPPED

3 TABLESPOONS COARSELY CHOPPED ITALIAN PARSLEY

SALT AND FRESHLY GROUND BLACK PEPPER

1⅓ CUPS GREEK YOGURT

1 TABLESPOON SHELLED PISTACHIO NUTS, CHOPPED

This is the way my friend Annette makes her beet salad. I love the colors here. And its freshness, even though it looks mayonnaisy; it's a surprise to remember that it's actually much lighter than it looks.

This is wonderful with fresh, roasted beets, or you can also use canned beets, in which case it will only take a second to put together. If you are using fresh ones and they have leaves, you can boil those too for a few minutes and dress them with olive oil to serve.

If using fresh, cut the leaves well above the bulb so that they don't bleed.

Preheat the oven to 350°F. Wash the (fresh) beets well, being careful not to pierce their skins. Wrap each fresh beet individually in aluminum foil and bake for about 1 hour, until tender when tested with a sharp knife.

Whip the oil lightly in a bowl with the lemon juice and garlic.

Wearing kitchen gloves, peel the beets. Trim away the root and cut them into nice chunks. If you are using canned beets, rinse if necessary and trim away any tough end bits and cut into chunks. Put in a bowl. Add the lemon oil, parsley and season with salt and pepper. Add the yogurt and mix gently. Scatter the pistachio nuts on top and serve.

SALATA HORIATIKI GREEK SALAD

Χωριάτικη

SERVES 2 TO 4

SERVES 2 TO 4

8 GORGEOUS SMALL RIPE TOMATOES, QUARTERED

1 CUCUMBER, SLICED THICKLY ON THE DIAGONAL

1 SMALL–MEDIUM RED ONION, SLICED

ABOUT 17 DRAINED KALAMATA OLIVES IN BRINE

1 HEAPING TABLESPOON CAPERS

2 SMALL HANDFULS OF PURSLANE IF YOU CAN GET IT

SALT AND FRESHLY GROUND BLACK PEPPER

5½-OUNCE SLAB OF FETA

1 TEASPOON OR SO DRIED OREGANO

¼ CUP OLIVE OIL

1 TABLESPOON RED WINE VINEGAR, OPTIONAL

The quality of tomatoes, olive oil and the other ingredients is really important to make the kind of salad at home that one will have eaten on vacation near a sun-soaked beach.

You can add a handful of other greens instead of the purslane (glistrida), if you like, but the padded thickness of their leaves is great, or just leave it plain. Many Greeks use only olive oil to dress their salads, while others add a little red wine vinegar. The juices at the bottom of the bowl are enjoyed and bread is used for "papara," the soaking of bread in the juices before eating. In some places in Greece they serve a dollop of mizithra cheese on top instead of feta.

Put the tomatoes, cucumber, onion, olives and capers into a serving bowl. Add the purslane and season with a little salt and a few grinds of pepper. Put the feta on top and crumble the oregano over with your fingers. Drizzle the olive oil over, and the vinegar if using. Serve with bread.

SALATA MAROULI LETTUCE SALAD

Σαλάτα μαρούλι

SERVES 6 TO 8

14 OUNCES ROMAINE LETTUCE

2 TABLESPOONS CHOPPED DILL

1½ OUNCES GREEN ONION, OR RED ONION, SLICED

¼ CUP OLIVE OIL

JUICE OF ½ LARGE LEMON

SALT AND FRESHLY GROUND BLACK PEPPER

So plain yet so good, and it goes well with many things. One of the plain salads always available in Greece. Use best-quality extra virgin olive oil.

Rinse the lettuce, shake it dry, then shred the leaves. Pat them dry with paper towels. Put in a bowl with the dill and onion. Dress with the olive oil and lemon juice just before eating. Add salt and pepper and toss lightly.

TOMATOSALATA TOMATO SALAD

Ντοματοσαλάτα

SERVES 2 TO 4

2¼ POUNDS LOVELY RIPE JUICY TOMATOES (ABOUT 6)

½ CUP KALAMATA OLIVES

2 TABLESPOONS CAPERS

¼ CUP OLIVE OIL

SALT AND FRESHLY GROUND BLACK PEPPER

1 TEASPOON DRIED OREGANO

In Greece a whole big beautiful tomato could make a meal, as it's so good on its own, just with a little salt and olive oil. A salad like this works well next to grilled foods such as bifteki.

Cut the tomatoes into nice chunks. Put them into a bowl with the olives, capers and olive oil, and season to taste with salt and pepper. Crumble the oregano over. Toss gently, and serve.

PATATOSALATA
POTATO SALAD

Πατατοσαλάτα

This salad goes very well with all grilled fish dishes. You could also add a couple of hard-boiled eggs here. Use lemon juice instead of the vinegar if you prefer.

SERVES 4 TO 6

1¾ POUND UNPEELED POTATOES

4 ANCHOVY FILLETS, ROUGHLY CHOPPED

¼ CUP KALAMATA OLIVES

2 TABLESPOONS CAPERS

2–3 TRIMMED GREEN ONIONS INCLUDING SOME GREEN PARTS, SLICED

¼ CUP COARSELY CHOPPED ITALIAN PARSLEY

ABOUT 6 TABLESPOONS OLIVE OIL

ABOUT 2 TABLESPOONS RED WINE VINEGAR

FRESHLY GROUND BLACK PEPPER

Boil the potatoes in salted water until tender but not too soft. Drain, and leave to cool for 10 minutes or so before pulling the skins away. Cut up into good chunks and put into a serving bowl. Add the anchovy, olives, capers, onions, parsley, olive oil and vinegar, and season with pepper. Toss gently, trying not to break up the potatoes. Taste for salt and serve warm or at room temperature. Even nice served cold the next day.

SALATA POLITIKI CABBAGE + PEPPER SALAD

Σαλάτα πολίτικη

SERVES MANY, MANY

2 POUNDS 10 OUNCES
CABBAGE (ABOUT
1 SMALL CABBAGE)

14 OUNCES CARROTS,
COARSELY SHREDDED

14 OUNCES SMALL GREEN
SWEET PEPPERS, SLICED

14 OUNCES SMALL RED
SWEET PEPPERS, SLICED

1¾ OUNCES GREEK CELERY
(OR THIN YOUNG CELERY
RIBS WITH SOME LEAVES),
CHOPPED

6 OUNCES RED WINE
VINEGAR

3 TABLESPOONS SALT

3 GARLIC CLOVES,
CHOPPED

GENEROUS PINCH OF
GROUND CHILE

OLIVE OIL, FOR SERVING

LEMON QUARTERS,
FOR SERVING, OPTIONAL

If this amount seems crazy, then just make half a portion. It's a lovely huge amount to make and it keeps well in the fridge, covered, for 5 to 6 days after it has been made. It will need a few days first in the fridge to drag out the juices before you can eat it. The red and green peppers used for this are the small, long and thin Greek ones.

Discard the outer leaves of the cabbage. Halve and core it, then shred medium-fine. Put in a large bowl with everything else except the olive oil and lemons. Roll up your sleeves and mix and knead everything together well with your hands. It needs a lot of pressing about. Cover and leave in the fridge for 3 days before tasting. But in the meantime, mix it each day to drag all the juices out.

Serve the salad drizzled with olive oil and a squeeze of lemon juice if you like.

Τιμολόγιον

ΚΑΦΕΣ	0.60
ΚΑΚΑΟ	0.60
ΤΕΪΟΝ	0.60
ΓΛΥΚΑ κουτ.	0.60
ΛΕΜΟΝΑΔΑ	0.60
ΠΟΡΤΟΚΑΛ.	0.60
ΚΟΚΑ-ΚΟΛΑ	0.60
ΠΕΨΙ-ΚΟΛΑ	0.60
ΟΥΖΟ ταρ.	
ΜΠΥΡΑ	0.90
ΚΡΑΣΙ	1
ΣΟΔΑ	0.60

Γ. ΟΙΚΟΝΟΜΟΥ

MAYIREFTA

READY-COOKED FOODS

There are some restaurants in Greece that only serve mayirefta (cooked) foods, and these will be all the dishes that need a long time in the oven and can't be prepared then and there to order. The Greek tapsi is something wonderful. Something vital. Tapsi is a roasting dish, often used to refer to a quantity—1 tapsi of this or that—and it has a wonderful connotation in Greece. There is something very encouraging about large tapsis, and large families everywhere.

PSARI FOURNOU ALA SPETSIOTA BAKED FISH WITH TOMATO

Ψάρι α λα σπετσιώτα

SERVES 4

4 7-OUNCE OR SO THICK, FIRM, SKINLESS WHITE FISH FILLETS

3 TABLESPOONS OLIVE OIL

JUICE OF 2 LEMONS

¼ CUP WHITE WINE

3 GARLIC CLOVES, CHOPPED

14-OUNCE CAN CHOPPED TOMATOES

1½ OUNCES CELERY RIBS WITH LEAVES, CHOPPED

¼ CUP CHOPPED ITALIAN PARSLEY

SALT AND FRESHLY GROUND BLACK PEPPER

OLIVE OIL, FOR SERVING

Bass, snapper, grouper or perch are good here. This is so simple to prepare you will hardly believe it. You will need an oven dish that will hold the fish fillets in a single layer, so of course, with a bigger dish you can up the ingredients. This is nice served with boiled potatoes, also showered with chopped parsley and a drizzle of olive oil. Use celery tops with many of the leaves rather than ribs. You might like to add a little chopped chile to the sauce as well.

Preheat the oven to 350°F. Season the fish fillets with a little salt. In a bowl mix the olive oil, lemon juice, wine, garlic, tomato, celery and 3 tablespoons of the parsley. Season with salt and pepper. Splatter a few tablespoons over the bottom of a baking dish large enough to hold the fillets comfortably in a single layer. Lay the fish fillets on top and pour over the rest of the tomato mixture. Bake, uncovered, for 45 to 55 minutes, depending on your fish. The sauce should be reduced and the tomato chunks starting to caramelize on the top. If the sauce is still watery, turn the oven off and prop the door open for 10 minutes. Drizzle with a little olive oil, scatter with the remaining parsley and serve with bread.

ARNI YUVETSI BAKED LAMB WITH RICE-SHAPED PASTA

Αρνί γιουβέτσι

SERVES 6

3 POUNDS 5 OUNCES LEG OF LAMB

½ LEMON

½ CUP OLIVE OIL

1 TEASPOON SWEET PAPRIKA

2 GARLIC CLOVES, FINELY CHOPPED

SALT AND FRESHLY GROUND BLACK PEPPER

5½ OUNCES GREEN ONIONS (ABOUT 4), QUARTERED AND COARSELY CHOPPED

14-OUNCE CAN CRUSHED TOMATOES

½ TEASPOON DRIED OREGANO

1 CINNAMON STICK

9 OUNCES KRITHARAKI OR RISONI (RICE-SHAPED DRIED PASTA)

SHREDDED KEFALOTIRI OR FIRM MIZITHRA CHEESE, FOR SERVING

Yuvetsi is traditionally a Sunday dish. People would put all their ingredients into the "yuvetsi" (the large ceramic dish that this is cooked in) and take it to the baker's with the package of kritharaki pasta. You could give any specific instructions to the baker, and he would add the pasta in at the end. Discussions would always be that the baker had done well that time, or perhaps it got a bit overcooked—but always it was good. And it would always smell like a whole tavern, having caught all the other interesting smells, like roasting chickens, in the air. This was a good way for the housewife to rest on a Sunday, and one of the family members, such as her husband or son, would go and collect the yuvetsi. If you don't have a yuvetsi, you can use a good wide, round or rectangular oven dish, and if you can't get the small rice-shaped pasta, you can use another type. This dish is often also made with beef, chicken or octopus. Sometimes the pasta is cooked with no meat, just tomato and coarsely grated firm mizithra.

Preheat the oven to 350°F. Trim any excess fat off the lamb. Squeeze the lemon juice over and massage it in. Put 4 tablespoons of the olive oil in a large (about 14¼ inches in diameter) baking dish (or a yuvetsi, of course, if you have one). Add the lamb, then drizzle the rest of the oil over it. Rub the paprika and garlic onto the lamb and season well with salt and pepper. Add the onions, tomatoes, oregano and cinnamon to the dish and sprinkle with some salt too. Put in the oven and roast for 30 minutes. Add 1 cup of hot water

continued

and cook for 1 hour, turning the lamb halfway through.

In the meantime, boil the pasta in lightly salted water until just done. Drain. When the lamb is done, add the pasta around it in the dish with 1½ cups of hot water and gently mix into the tomato, trying not to get the pasta on the lamb. Return to the oven for 10 to 15 minutes, or until the pasta has absorbed quite a bit of the liquid but is still nice and saucy. Remove from the oven and rest in a warm spot for 5 minutes. Grind a little pepper over and take the whole dish to the table for serving, with the cheese on the side for whoever wants.

ARNI MASTELO LAMB IN A FLOWERPOT WITH DILL + RED WINE

Αρνι μαστέλο

SERVES 6

A FEW DRY GRAPEVINE BRANCHES

A LARGE HANDFUL OF DILL, STALKS AND LEAVES TOGETHER

2 SHOULDERS OF LAMB (ABOUT 3¾ POUNDS TOTAL WITH BONE), CUT INTO LARGE CHUNKS BY YOUR BUTCHER

SALT AND FRESHLY GROUND BLACK PEPPER

2 TABLESPOONS OLIVE OIL

2 CUPS RED WINE

A NICE HANDFUL OF CHOPPED DILL, FOR SERVING

I love this for its simplicity. And for the very fact that it's cooked in a flowerpot (with no hole in the bottom!). On Sifnos, the lamb is slowly cooked with red wine, flavored with dill or fennel, over dried vines in a clay "mastelo" or pot. A few vine branches are arranged in a criss-cross pattern to form a grid on the base of the pot. This adds flavor to the lamb and makes it tender. You can use an ordinary ceramic dish if you don't have a suitable flowerpot. Preferably with a lid and roughly 9½ inches in diameter.

Preheat the oven to 400°F. Arrange 2 or 3 vine branches (breaking them up if necessary) over the bottom of a wide terra-cotta pot about 9½ inches in diameter and 4 inches high. If yours is much wider, you may need to add a bit more wine. Put some of the dill in too. Rinse the lamb or wipe the pieces all over with a damp paper towel. Lay them on top of the branches, layering the dill and salting and peppering as you go. Drizzle in the oil and pour in the wine. Cover with a lid or several layers of aluminum foil and bake for 2 to 2½ hours, turning the lamb and basting a couple of times. The lamb should be melting soft and there will be quite a bit of sauce. If you are not serving immediately, turn the oven off and leave the pot in, still covered, while it cools.

Serve with a little of the sauce drizzled over and scattered with the chopped dill. Nice with soft roasted or boiled potatoes.

ARNI FRICASSÉE LAMB WITH LETTUCE

Αρνί φρικασέ

SERVES 4

1 POUND 9 OUNCES ROMAINE LETTUCE (ABOUT 2)

7¾ OUNCES LARGE GREEN ONIONS (ABOUT 4)

3-POUND SHOULDER OF LAMB WITH BONE, CUT INTO LARGE EVEN CHUNKS (ROUGHLY 2–2½ INCHES) BY YOUR BUTCHER

½ CUP OLIVE OIL

3 GARLIC CLOVES, 2 CHOPPED, 1 WHOLE

¾ CUP WHITE WINE

SALT AND FRESHLY GROUND BLACK PEPPER

1½ CUPS HOT VEGETABLE BROTH, MADE WITH AN MSG-FREE BOUILLON CUBE, OR HOMEMADE STOCK

1 SMALL CELERY RIB, WELL CHOPPED

A PINCH OF GROUND CHILE

2 EGGS

JUICE OF 2 LEMONS

1 HEAPING TABLESPOON COARSELY CHOPPED DILL

1 TABLESPOON COARSELY CHOPPED MINT

The lettuce in this dish is often added to the pot and it's all cooked on the stove. Here the lamb is baked and the lettuce is softened separately in a pan, but the flavors all unite, nevertheless, on the plate.

The dish is finished with an egg and lemon sauce, very typical in Greece.

Preheat the oven to 350°F. Trim away the core of the lettuces and separate the leaves. Rinse and drain them, and shake off any excess water. Cut across the leaves into 1¼- to 1½-inch-wide strips and keep in a colander for now. Trim away the thick outer layer from the onions, but leave the green stems on. Quarter them lengthways so you have nice long pieces. Rinse and drain. Trim the lamb of any excess fat, but you can leave some of the nicer-looking fat on. Rinse and pat the pieces

dry with paper towels, making sure that there are no stray shards of bone.

Drizzle 5 tablespoons of the oil into a heatproof nonstick roasting dish about 12 × 8½ inches. Add the lamb, toss to coat with the oil and roast for 30 minutes. Turn the lamb over and roast for another 30 minutes. Add the onion, chopped garlic, wine, and salt and pepper to taste. Roast for a further 30 minutes, or until the lamb is browned and tender. Keep an eye on the onion and the garlic so that they do not burn. Add the broth and cook for another 10 minutes or so.

Meanwhile, heat the remaining oil in a large nonstick skillet. Add the whole garlic clove, celery and chile and sauté until the celery is softened and golden. Add the lettuce, pressing it all in. Sprinkle with salt and pepper, cover, and simmer for 10 to 12 minutes, or until the lettuce has wilted and all of the liquid has evaporated. Keep hot.

Whip the eggs in a bowl, then beat in the lemon juice. Sprinkle in a little salt. Remove the roasting dish from the oven and transfer the lamb and onion to a plate. Pour a cup of the hot liquid from the roasting dish into the egg and lemon juice mixture, beating well to acclimatize. Pour back into the roasting dish and put over the lowest possible heat, stirring and mixing constantly with a wooden spoon until the sauce thickens a little and has a creamy consistency. Remove from the heat. Return the lamb to the dish and shuffle the pieces to coat with the sauce. Make sure that the lettuce is hot, reheating if necessary. Stir in the dill and mint. Serve some lettuce on each plate with a couple of pieces of lamb and a drizzle of sauce over the top. Grind over some pepper and serve hot.

ISN'T IT LOVELY HOW OUZO CHANGES

from transparent to white when water or ice is added?

PATATES FOURNOU ME TOMATES ROAST TOMATO POTATOES

Πατάτες φούρνου με ντομάτες

SERVES 6

2 POUNDS 10 OUNCES POTATOES, PEELED AND RINSED

2 RIPE TOMATOES, CUT INTO CHUNKS

1 RED ONION, SLICED

6 TABLESPOONS OLIVE OIL

1 HEAPING TEASPOON DRIED OREGANO

Preheat the oven to 350°F. Halve the potatoes lengthwise, then cut each half into 2 or 3 wedges, depending on the size of your potatoes. Spread them in an 8½ × 12-inch nonstick baking dish. Scatter the tomatoes and onion over, drizzle with the olive oil, and add salt and black pepper generously. Crush the oregano between your fingers, letting it fall over the potatoes. Turn the potatoes to coat them well with everything. Drizzle 2 cups of water down the sides of the dish and shuffle it. Roast until the potatoes are tender and melting and the sauce is thick, about 1½ hours. Turn and baste the potatoes every 20 minutes or so and make sure that nothing is sticking to the bottom of the dish and no potatoes are out of the liquid too long and looking plasticy. Taste to see if it needs any salt and pepper. Serve hot.

PATATES FOURNOU LEMONATES ROAST LEMON POTATOES

Πατάτες φούρνου λεμονάτες

SERVES 6

2 POUNDS 10 OUNCES
POTATOES, PEELED
AND RINSED

JUICE OF 1 LARGE LEMON

6 TABLESPOONS OLIVE OIL

SALT AND FRESHLY GROUND
BLACK PEPPER

1 HEAPING TEASPOON
DRIED OREGANO

These are good with grilled foods. They are not crusty like regular roast potatoes, but soft and moist. You can add more lemon here depending on what you will be serving them with. I use a nonstick oven dish, about 8½ × 12 inches.

Preheat the oven to 350°F. Halve the potatoes lengthwise then cut each half into 2 or 3 wedges, depending on the size of your potatoes. Spread them in an 8½ × 12-inch nonstick baking dish. Splash the lemon juice and olive oil over them, and add salt and pepper generously. Crush the oregano between your fingers, letting it fall over the potatoes.

Turn the potatoes to coat them well with everything. Drizzle 2 cups of water down the sides of the dish and give it a shuffle.

Roast until the potatoes are tender and melting and a bit golden here and there with still a bit of sauce in the dish, about 1½ hours, turning and basting them every 20 minutes or so. Add more salt and pepper to taste and serve hot.

KOUNELI STIFADO RABBIT + ONION STEW

Κουνέλι στιφάδο

SERVES 4 TO 6

1 RABBIT (ABOUT 2¾ POUNDS), CLEANED, HEAD REMOVED

2¼ POUNDS SMALL BEAUTIFUL RED ONIONS OR SHALLOTS (ABOUT 1 OUNCE EACH)

10 TABLESPOONS OLIVE OIL

3 TABLESPOONS RED WINE VINEGAR

SALT AND FRESHLY GROUND BLACK PEPPER

1 CUP RED WINE

14-OUNCE CAN CRUSHED TOMATOES

2 BAY LEAVES

5 ALLSPICE BERRIES

1 CINNAMON STICK

This is often made with hare, which would need longer cooking time, and it is also wonderful with beef or octopus. It's nice and wintry and oniony and goes very well with just a dish of cooked wild greens.

Cut up the rabbit into about 12 pieces. Rinse, and pat dry well.

Peel the onions very carefully, as the tops and bottoms must remain intact to keep them whole when cooked. Rinse and drain, keeping them in a colander for now.

Preheat the oven to 350°F. Heat 4 tablespoons of the oil in a large nonstick skillet over medium heat. Add the pieces of rabbit and fry until nicely golden on all sides. Add the vinegar, season with salt and pepper and cook until reduced to a syrup. Add the wine and simmer for a few minutes before removing the pan from the heat.

Pour the remaining olive oil into a roasting dish about 13 inches in diameter, or a large rectangular one. Tip the rabbit and all the sauce from the skillet into the dish, arranging the rabbit over the bottom. Fill in any gaps between the pieces with the onions, then put the rest of the onions on top. Sprinkle some salt and pepper over these. Add the tomatoes, bay leaves, allspice and cinnamon, and 1 cup of water.

Bake, covered with aluminum foil, for 1 hour, checking once or twice that nothing is sticking. To loosen things, hold the edges of the dish with oven mitts and give it a good shuffle.

After an hour, shuffle the dish again and turn the onions over, covering them with some of the liquid. Lower the temperature to 315°F and bake for a further 50 minutes, checking and shuffling once or twice. The rabbit should be meltingly tender and the onions soft. Baste everything well. Turn the oven up to 400°F, remove the foil and roast for 10 minutes more to get a bit golden. Serve warm.

VREHI PAPADES KE KAREKLO-PODA-RA / IT'S RAIN-ING PRIESTS AND CHAIR LEGS

It was raining priests and chair legs in Mani (even though the atmosphere didn't need enhancing). We lunched on tomatoes and almost turquoise olive oil that must have been reflecting the Greek blues, and the onions were as sweet as peaches.

KOTOPOULO FOURNOU ROAST CHICKEN

Κοτόπουλο φούρνου

SERVES 4

1 3-POUND 5-OUNCE CHICKEN

2¼ POUNDS POTATOES (ABOUT 6 MEDIUM), PEELED, HALVED LENGTHWISE THEN HALVED OR QUARTERED AGAIN INTO WEDGES

3 GARLIC CLOVES, PEELED

2 BAY LEAVES

JUICE OF 2 JUICY LEMONS

SALT AND FRESHLY GROUND BLACK PEPPER

3 TEASPOONS DRIED OREGANO

6 TABLESPOONS OLIVE OIL

This is a basic, classic type of dish that you would find in many Greek homes. Simple to put together, rustic and very homemadey, left in the oven for a long while to get soft and gooey. You can use a large rectangular nonstick oven dish or a round one.

Preheat the oven to 315°F. Rinse the chicken and pat dry well with kitchen paper. Put breast down into a large roasting dish and scatter the potatoes around with the garlic cloves and bay leaves. Drizzle some lemon juice over the potatoes and inside the chicken, and rub the rest into the skin. Scatter salt and pepper and crumble some of the oregano into the chicken's cavity, then rub more salt and pepper and the rest of the oregano over the skin. Drizzle the oil over. Gently pour 1 cup of water around the edges. Roast, basting regularly, for 1½ hours. Now turn the chicken, breast side up, baste again and add ¼ cup of water. Return to the oven for 1 hour, basting a couple more times and turning the potatoes at least once so they don't dry out. Add ¼ cup of water 10 or 15 minutes from the end. The chicken should be moist, tender and have a crisp skin, while the potatoes should be moist and soft, not crisp. Rest the chicken for 5 minutes or so before cutting into servings.

KOKKORAS KRASSATOS WINED ROOSTER

Κόκορας κρασάτος

SERVES 4 TO 6

5 TABLESPOONS OLIVE OIL

1 ROOSTER WITH SKIN ON
(ABOUT 5 POUNDS), CUT
INTO 10 PIECES

2 RED ONIONS, CHOPPED

3 GARLIC CLOVES, CHOPPED

SALT AND FRESHLY GROUND
BLACK PEPPER

2 CUPS RED WINE

1 HEAPING TABLESPOON
TOMATO PASTE

14-OUNCE CAN CHOPPED
TOMATOES

½ CINNAMON STICK

2 BAY LEAVES

3 ALLSPICE BERRIES

HILOPITES (PAGE 248), OR
14 OUNCES DRIED FLAT
PASTA PIECES, FOR SERVING

SHREDDED FIRM MIZITHRA
CHEESE OR HARD SALTED
RICOTTA, FOR SERVING

This is a dish you may find in the villages of Greece. Quite wintry really. It is lovely with homemade noodles (or bought dried ones). It is also often served with french fries instead of noodles.

You can use a chicken here in place of the rooster, but the cooking time will be shorter.

Heat the olive oil in a large nonstick pan with high sides over medium heat and fry the rooster pieces until golden on all sides. Add the onions around the rooster and fry, stirring often, until it is golden, then add the garlic. Season well with salt and pepper on both sides. When it smells good, add the wine.

Simmer uncovered and when much of the wine has evaporated, add the tomato paste, the tomatoes and a tomato can of water. Add the cinnamon, bay leaves and allspice, and a little more salt. Bring to a boil, cover, then reduce the heat to low and simmer for about 2 hours, or until the bird is very tender but not falling off the bone. Add a little more water toward the end if the sauce needs loosening up–there must be some nice thickened sauce to serve with the noodles. Turn off the heat and leave, covered.

Cook the hilopites in boiling salted water until soft, a couple of minutes, or follow the package instructions. Drain and toss with a little of the sauce. Serve right away, with pieces of rooster on top of the pasta, a little more sauce over and a scattering of cheese.

HILOPITES HOMEMADE NOODLES

Χυλοπίτες

SERVES 4

2 CUPS ALL-PURPOSE FLOUR

½ TEASPOON SALT

2 EGGS, LIGHTLY BEATEN

1 TABLESPOON OLIVE OIL

3–4 TABLESPOONS MILK

Here is a version if you decide to make your own noodles/pasta. See the egg-free, milk-free version suitable for fasting on page 81.

These vary in shape, sometimes square and sometimes longer rectangles. The pasta is often well cooked, and there is something wonderfully Greek about this.

Put the flour, salt, eggs, olive oil and 3 tablespoons of the milk in a bowl and mix well. Knead with lightly floured hands to a firm, smooth dough, adding a little more flour or milk as needed. Wrap in a cloth and leave it for at least half an hour at room temperature.

Divide the dough into quarters. Keeping the others covered, roll one out as thinly as possible, until almost see-through. You might need to let it rest and relax every so often before continuing to roll some more. Leave each sheet of dough on the counter while you roll the rest. Starting with the first rolled sheet, cut it into ⅝-inch-wide strips, and then into rough rectangles. Leave them out on a lightly floured tray while you cut all the sheets. They can be cooked right away or left to partially dry, and they can be totally dried but may become fragile.

Put into a large pot of boiling salted water and cook until tender, a couple of minutes. Drain and serve.

YUVARLAKIA DILLED MEATBALLS

Γιουβαρλάκια

SERVES 5 OR 6

14 OUNCES GROUND BEEF

14 OUNCES GROUND PORK

1 EGG, LIGHTLY BEATEN

½ CUP MEDIUM-GRAIN RICE

½ TEASPOON GROUND
ALLSPICE

5 TABLESPOONS COARSELY
CHOPPED DILL

5 TABLESPOONS COARSELY
CHOPPED ITALIAN PARSLEY

1 LARGE RED ONION,
GRATED ON THE LARGE
HOLES OF A GRATER

2 TABLESPOONS OLIVE OIL

5¼ OUNCES MILK

SALT AND FRESHLY GROUND
BLACK PEPPER

3 TABLESPOONS EACH
CHOPPED DILL AND
PARSLEY STALKS

⅔ CUP SHELLED PEAS
(ABOUT 10½ OUNCES
UNSHELLED)

2 TABLESPOONS CHOPPED
ITALIAN PARSLEY, EXTRA

1 TABLESPOON CHOPPED
DILL, EXTRA

2 EGGS

JUICE OF 2 LEMONS

This is a lovely dilly brothy dish to be eaten with a spoon. I use a large cast-iron pot, but a high-sided nonstick pan is good, too. I love this with some peas, but the traditional way is without.

Mix the beef, pork, egg, rice, allspice, dill, parsley, onion, olive oil and milk in a nice big bowl and add pepper and 1 teaspoon of salt. Knead very well. Break off pieces of about 1½ ounces, and roll them into compact balls.

Heat a large pot and add the meatballs in 2 batches with no oil. Put the lid on and cook on high heat until the color of the meatballs changes and they firm up enough for you to turn them. When their undersides are lightly golden, turn them. Cook until golden all over, then transfer to a plate. Do the next batch, add all back to the pot and cook until golden. Add 6 cups of water, about ½ teaspoon of salt and a little pepper, and the dill and parsley stalks. Cover and simmer gently for about 50 minutes. The meatballs will look like hedgehogs and that's the way they are, but if you boil them too hard, they might break up. Add the peas and simmer until tender but still green, about 10 minutes; it must be nice and brothy (you will still be adding the egg and lemon sauce), so add a little more hot water as you think necessary. Add the extra parsley and dill, then turn off the heat.

Whisk the eggs and lemon juice in a bowl with ½ teaspoon of salt. Add a ladleful of the meatball broth, whisk in to acclimatize, then add another ladleful. Pour it back into the pot and gently stir with a wooden spoon. Leave for a minute or two for the sauce to thicken a bit, holding the pot and shuffling. Taste for salt. Serve warm, with a good grind of pepper.

SOUTZOUKAKIA CUMIN MEATBALLS IN TOMATO

Σουτζουκάκια

SERVES 4 TO 6

3½ OUNCES CRUSTLESS BREAD (ABOUT 3 SLICES), TORN UP

¾ CUP MILK

1 POUND 9 OUNCES GROUND BEEF

1 EGG, LIGHTLY BEATEN

2 TEASPOONS GROUND CUMIN

2 TABLESPOONS CHOPPED ITALIAN PARSLEY

3 GARLIC CLOVES, 2 FINELY CHOPPED, 1 WHOLE

SALT AND FRESHLY GROUND BLACK PEPPER

7 TABLESPOONS OLIVE OIL

2 14-OUNCE CANS CRUSHED TOMATOES

½ CUP RED WINE

This is often served with rice, mashed potatoes or even french fries, which is how I love it. It is a dish that came from Smyrni in Asia Minor when it was part of Greece (now Izmir, Turkey).

The cumin is fabulous here. If possible, try and grind the cumin seeds in a spice grinder.

Put the bread into a bowl, cover with the milk and leave it for about 10 minutes to soak and soften.

In another bowl put the beef, egg, cumin, parsley, chopped garlic, and season with salt and pepper. Squeeze out excess milk from the bread and add the bread to the beef. Mix in very well with a wooden spoon and then with your hands. Form into elongated meatballs of about 1¾ ounces each. Line them up on a tray.

Heat 3 tablespoons of the olive oil in a nonstick pot, add the whole clove of garlic, and when it begins to smell good, add the tomatoes. Season with salt and a little pepper, put the lid on and simmer for 10 minutes or so, smoothing out any big lumpy tomato pieces. Heat the remaining olive oil in a large nonstick skillet that has a lid. Add the soutzoukakia (they should all just fit if you have a

big skillet). Cook until golden
all over, gently turning them
with tongs or by flicking the pan
sharply from your wrist if you
can manage. When they are nice
and gently browned, add the
wine and cook for 5 to 6 minutes
on high heat, until it reduces.
Scrape the tomato sauce over the
meatballs and bring it to a gentle
boil. Lower the heat slightly, put
the lid on and simmer for about
20 minutes. Shuffle the skillet
once or twice to make sure
nothing is sticking. There should
be a good amount of sauce at
the end. Remove from the heat.
Leave with the lid on for a few
minutes or so before serving.

POLI VARI KE OHI—STRONG BUT NOT

For example . . . when you order a Greek coffee, or someone could be "Poli omorfi ke ohi": beautiful but not. One understands exactly what one means.

PASTITSIO
BEEF, MACARONI +
BÉCHAMEL LAYERS

Παστίτσιο

SERVES 9 TO 12

MEAT SAUCE

5 TABLESPOONS OLIVE OIL

2 LARGE RED ONIONS, GRATED ON THE LARGE HOLES OF A GRATER

1¾ POUND GROUND BEEF

7 OUNCES GROUND PORK

2 GARLIC CLOVES, CHOPPED

3 WHOLE CLOVES

3 ALLSPICE BERRIES

1 CUP RED WINE

14-OUNCE CAN CHOPPED TOMATOES

1 TABLESPOON TOMATO PASTE

2 TABLESPOONS CHOPPED ITALIAN PARSLEY

SALT AND FRESHLY GROUND BLACK PEPPER

14 OUNCES LONG THIN MACARONI

1½ OUNCES SHREDDED MIZITHRA CHEESE OR SALTED RICOTTA

This large tapsi (dish) should give you leftovers for the next day. It can even be made the day before and heated to serve.

The macaroni mainly used in Greece is about 10 inches long, with a diameter of about ⅛ inch and a hole down the middle. Use something similar if you can't get this exact one.

This is Roulla's pastitsio. She is a lovely lady, and great cook, in Mani. Nikos' mother and Emily's mother-in-law. Roulla said she cooks the whole package of macaroni anyway, and then she scoops out the extra and gives it to her husband with some shredded mizithra. Probably she's not hungry after tasting her meat sauce and all the rest of her preparations.

For the meat sauce, heat the oil in a large nonstick skillet that has a lid. Add the onions, beef and pork and fry over high heat until all the moisture goes. Add the garlic, cloves and allspice and when that smells good, add the wine. Cook until most of it has evaporated, then add the tomatoes, tomato paste and parsley, and season well with salt and pepper. Stir in 2 cups of hot water. Put the lid on, lower the heat and simmer for about 45 minutes. You want a compact, almost dry sauce, so take the lid off for the last 10 minutes if you need to reduce it. Taste for seasoning, put the lid back on and set aside.

Cook the macaroni in boiling salted water till just done. Drain well by shaking the colander and pressing on the pasta, and if necessary use paper towels to soak up any water that's left. Put into the bottom of a 10½ × 13½-inch baking dish that is at least 2¾ inches high. Add the shredded mizithra, mixing it through the macaroni. Press the pasta down firmly because it needs to be as compact as possible for slicing later.

Preheat the oven to 350°F. For the béchamel, heat the milk, cinnamon and cloves in a large saucepan. Melt the butter in a large wide pot. Add the flour and stir with a wooden spoon on low heat until smooth, then add warm milk bit by bit, stirring all the time. Now whisk, and when you have a lump-free thick cream, remove from the heat. It's important that it be thick and gloopy on the surface. Break the eggs into a bowl and whisk well. Whisk a ladleful of béchamel into the eggs to acclimatize them, then whisk them into the sauce. Add the shredded cheese and taste for salt and pepper.

Scrape the meat sauce over the pasta in a good level layer and press it down firmly. Pour the béchamel over the top. Bake for 30 to 40 minutes or until the béchamel is firm and golden brown on top. Remove from the oven and allow to cool for about 45 minutes before serving, so that the layers become firm enough to slice. If you try to serve it earlier, it may not hold its shape and may ooze. This is great the next day also.

BÉCHAMEL

8 CUPS MILK

½ TEASPOON GROUND CINNAMON

¼ TEASPOON GROUND CLOVES

1 CUP (2 STICKS) SWEET BUTTER

1⅔ CUPS ALL-PURPOSE FLOUR

3 EGGS

2¾ OUNCES MIZITHRA CHEESE OR HARD SALTED RICOTTA, COARSELY SHREDDED

MOUSSAKA

Μουσακάς

2¼ POUNDS EGGPLANTS

1 POUND 7 OUNCES ZUCCHINI

MEAT SAUCE

5 TABLESPOONS OLIVE OIL

1¾ POUND GROUND BEEF

7 OUNCES GROUND PORK

2 LARGE RED ONIONS, GRATED ON THE LARGE HOLES OF A GRATER

2 GARLIC CLOVES, CHOPPED

3 WHOLE CLOVES

3 ALLSPICE BERRIES

1 CUP RED WINE

14-OUNCE CAN CHOPPED TOMATOES

1 TABLESPOON TOMATO PASTE

2 TABLESPOONS CHOPPED ITALIAN PARSLEY

SALT AND FRESHLY GROUND BLACK PEPPER

LIGHT OLIVE OIL, FOR FRYING

This is a nice huge amount—a good dishful that will give you plenty, even for next day. You can even freeze some portions. If this dish seems like too much work all in one go, you can make the meat sauce the day before. The wonderful thing that Roulla taught me here is to use olive oil instead of butter in the béchamel. Use a good-tasting olive oil, but you can still use butter if you prefer. I like this when the béchamel is like a duvet covering a bed of ground meat and fried eggplant and zucchini. Although it is known as a fairly heavy dish, you don't have to eat a huge portion.

Cut the eggplants lengthwise into slices about ¼ inch thick. Sprinkle with salt and leave in a colander for ½ hour for the juices to drain. Slice the zucchini slightly thinner, also lengthwise.

To make the meat sauce, heat the oil in a large nonstick skillet with a lid. Add the beef, pork and onions and fry until lightly brown and the moisture has gone. Add the garlic, cloves and allspice and when that smells good, add the wine. Simmer until most of it has evaporated. Add the tomatoes, tomato paste and parsley. Season well with salt and pepper. Stir in a tomato can of water. Put the lid on and simmer for 1 hour, taking the lid off in the last 10 minutes if it looks liquidy (it needs to be fairly dry for the moussaka). Remove the cloves and allspice if you find them, then taste for seasoning.

Meanwhile, fry the eggplant and zucchini. Rinse the eggplant and dry very well with paper towels. Heat very little olive oil in a large nonstick skillet and fry the eggplant slices in batches. When the fried side is golden, flip the slices over and prick with a fork, especially where they may still be hard. Press the slices with the fork and they will soften some more. When they are golden, remove to a plate lined with a couple of layers of paper towels and sprinkle with salt. Continue until all the eggplant is done, adding as little olive oil to the skillet as necessary. Fry the zucchini in the same way.

For the béchamel, heat the milk with the cinnamon and cloves in a saucepan and keep warm. Heat the oil in a large wide pot on low heat. Stir the flour in with a wooden spoon and continue stirring until smooth to cook it a bit. Add the warm milk bit by bit, stirring with the wooden spoon at first, then changing to a whisk to give you a lump-free, thick béchamel (it's important that it be thick and gloopy on the surface).

Remove from the heat. Break the eggs into a bowl and whisk well. Add a good ladleful of béchamel to acclimatize them, then whisk them into the béchamel. Add the mizithra and whisk to incorporate. Add a good grind of pepper and taste for salt.

Preheat the oven to 350°F. Layer the eggplant on the bottom of a 13½ × 10½-inch baking dish, leaving no gaps. Layer the zucchini on top. Scrape the meat sauce over the vegetables, patting it down and smoothing the top to make a firm mattress for the béchamel to lie on. Spoon the béchamel on top and level the surface. Bake for 30 to 40 minutes or until the béchamel is firm and golden. Allow to cool and set for about 45 minutes before cutting. If you try to serve it earlier, it may not hold its shape and may ooze.

BÉCHAMEL

8 CUPS MILK

½ TEASPOON CINNAMON

¼ TEASPOON GROUND CLOVES

1 CUP OLIVE OIL

1⅔ CUPS ALL-PURPOSE FLOUR

3 EGGS

2¾ OUNCES MIZITHRA CHEESE OR HARD SALTED RICOTTA, COARSELY SHREDDED

TOMATES YEMISTES STUFFED TOMATOES

Ντομάτες γεμιστές

MAKES 12

12 LOVELY RIPE TOMATOES (ABOUT 5¾ OUNCES EACH)

1 CUP TOMATO SAUCE

1 TEASPOON SUGAR

SALT AND FRESHLY GROUND BLACK PEPPER

10 TABLESPOONS OLIVE OIL

5 OUNCES GREEN ONIONS WITH SOME GREEN, CHOPPED

1½ OUNCES CELERY WITH LEAVES, CHOPPED

2 GARLIC CLOVES, CHOPPED

⅔ CUP MEDIUM-GRAIN RICE

3 TABLESPOONS COARSELY CHOPPED ITALIAN PARSLEY

1 POUND 5 OUNCES POTATOES, PEELED, HALVED LENGTHWISE, EACH HALF CUT INTO 3 OR 4 WEDGES

1½ TABLESPOONS BUTTER

This is often done with a mixture of different vegetables, such as large zucchini and bell peppers. Here I have done only tomatoes. You may need to adjust cooking times or water amounts, as it will depend entirely on the tomatoes, but you need to cook this until there is only some thickened gooey liquid at the bottom of the dish, and the tomatoes are tender and roasty but not falling apart and the potatoes soft. I use a big round oven dish about 13½ inches in diameter. The tomatoes are lovely served with a dollop of yogurt on the side (page 131, with or without the mint and paprika) and a green salad.

Top the tomatoes, keeping their hats aside for now. Scoop out the insides using a sharp knife and a sharp spoon. Take care not to pierce the shells. Put the pulp into a food processor or blender and pulse it to a thick juice. To this add the tomato sauce, sugar and a little salt and pepper, and mix.

Preheat the oven to 325°F. Heat 5 tablespoons of the olive oil in a medium pan over medium heat and sauté the onion until softened. Add the celery and sauté on low heat until it is soft. Add the garlic and when it smells good, add 2 cups of the tomato mixture. Bring to a boil, then stir in the rice. Add enough water, ¼ to ½ cup, to prevent the mixture sticking. Cook for 7 to 8 minutes. Remove from the heat and stir in the parsley.

Sprinkle the cavity of the tomatoes with a little salt. Fill each one two-thirds full with the rice mixture and put their hats on. Arrange the tomatoes in a baking dish large enough to hold them with the potatoes. Scatter the potatoes around, propping up any leaning tomatoes if necessary, and pour the remaining tomato mixture over here and there. Drizzle the rest of the olive oil over the top of the tomatoes and sprinkle salt on the potatoes as well as on the tops of the tomatoes (some people like to sprinkle a little sugar on here, too). Dot the butter on the tomatoes and finally, pour 1 cup of water gently around the potatoes. Bake for about 1½ hours, turning the potatoes over and basting 3 or 4 times. Add a little more water if the sauce becomes too dry during this time, but this will depend entirely on your tomatoes. The finished dish should have some thickened sauce on the bottom.

PAPOUTSAKIA SMALL SHOES

Παπουτσάκια

These are basically the same ingredients as moussaka, but prepared differently and served in individual "shoe servings."

SERVES 8

4 LONG EGGPLANTS (ABOUT 9 OUNCES EACH), ALL OF THE SAME DIMENSIONS

ABOUT ½ CUP OLIVE OIL

1 LARGE RED ONION, CHOPPED

14 OUNCES GROUND BEEF

2 GARLIC CLOVES, FINELY CHOPPED

½ CUP RED WINE

2 14-OUNCE CANS CRUSHED TOMATOES

¼ CUP CHOPPED ITALIAN PARSLEY

SALT AND FRESHLY GROUND BLACK PEPPER

BÉCHAMEL

3 TABLESPOONS BUTTER

7 TABLESPOONS ALL-PURPOSE FLOUR

10½ OUNCES MILK, HEATED

A LARGE PINCH OF NUTMEG

SALT AND FRESHLY GROUND BLACK PEPPER

3 TABLESPOONS SHREDDED KEFALOTIRI CHEESE

Cut the eggplants in half lengthwise, sprinkle the cut sides with salt and leave them upside-down in a colander for half an hour or so to drain away any bitter juices. Drizzle some oil into a large non-stick skillet over medium heat and when hot, add half the eggplant halves. Fry until deep golden and soft on both sides and when you prick the thickest part with a fork there is no resistance. Remove to a platter and fry the remaining eggplant halves. When cooled, scoop out the flesh using a sharp spoon, leaving a ¼- to ⅜-inch border. Chop the flesh and put aside. Wipe out the skillet. Add 3 tablespoons of olive oil to it and sauté the onion until golden. Add the beef and fry until browned. Add the garlic, cook for a moment more until it smells good, then add the wine and let it simmer for a minute or two. Add 1 can of tomatoes and the parsley, and season with salt and pepper. Cook, stirring a couple of times, for about 20 minutes, or until thickened. Add the chopped eggplant and simmer for another 10 or 12 minutes, or until most of the liquid has gone.

Preheat the oven to 350°F. To make the béchamel, melt the butter in a heavy-bottomed saucepan over low heat and stir in the flour. Whisk the milk in gradually to ensure no lumps. Add the nutmeg and season with salt and a little pepper. Whisk until thick.

Empty the remaining can of tomatoes over the bottom of a 10½ × 13½-inch roasting dish and add a little salt. Line up the eggplant shells on top, cut side up, and sprinkle with salt. Divide the meat mixture among them. Dollop 2 to 3 tablespoons of béchamel on each, scatter some kefalotiri over and pour ½ cup of water around them. Bake until roasty and golden on top, about 30 minutes.

LAHANODOLMADES CABBAGE ROLLS

Λαχανοντολμάδες

MAKES ABOUT 21

3½ POUNDS SAVOY CABBAGE (ABOUT 1 LARGE)

7 OUNCES GROUND PORK

7 OUNCES GROUND BEEF

1 CUP MEDIUM-GRAIN RICE

1 LARGE RED ONION, GRATED ON THE LARGE HOLES OF A GRATER

14-OUNCE CAN CRUSHED TOMATOES

¼ CUP CHOPPED ITALIAN PARSLEY

1 TEASPOON SWEET PAPRIKA

4 LEMONS

SALT AND FRESHLY GROUND BLACK PEPPER

3 TABLESPOONS BUTTER

¼ CUP OLIVE OIL

4 EGGS

This is wonderful. Although it may seem complicated, it's quite simple. You will need a big and wide pot to hold the bundles and a plate inverted into the pot to hold the bundles in place.

It's difficult to judge the exact amount of cabbage and filling here; it depends on how many untorn leaves you get from your cabbage. If you happen to end up with some spare filling, you can cook it on the stove with some water as an extra side. I love the savoy cabbage, but you can use any type with big flat leaves.

This is not a dish that keeps very well, as the sauce makes it difficult to warm up, so if you think this makes more than you'll need at one sitting, halve the recipe.

Carefully remove the cabbage leaves one by one with a small sharp knife, taking care not to break them. Rinse in cold water, then boil in a large pot of boiling salted water in batches for just a few minutes, until softened.

Gently remove the leaves and put the cooking water aside for later. Don't discard the tough outer leaves or torn ones because they will be used later to line the cooking pot, and the smaller inner leaves can be used for any patching up. You will need about 21 good leaves. Rinse these under cold water, shake off the excess, then lay them flat on trays lined with clean dish cloths. Cut away any thick bottom stems if they look like they won't roll up easily.

In a bowl, mix together the pork, beef, rice (uncooked), onion, tomatoes, parsley, paprika and juice of 1 lemon, and season well with salt and a few grinds of pepper. Spoon a healthy wooden spoonful (about 1¾ ounces) of mixture onto the lower middle of each leaf. Start rolling up the filling from the bottom. Make one full turn, tuck both sides toward the middle, then continue rolling. Don't roll too tightly, as the rice will expand during cooking, but they must be compact to hold their bundles.

Heat half the butter and half the oil in a large wide nonstick pot that has a lid. Line the bottom with the reserved outer cabbage leaves. Arrange the cabbage rolls tightly on top in concentric circles, starting from the outside. When one layer is full, make another on top until all the rolls are in. Dot the rest of the butter on top and drizzle the remaining oil over. Sprinkle lightly with salt and pepper. Pour in enough of the reserved cabbage water to just cover, about 3 cups. Find a plate that fits into the pot snugly and put it on top, inverted, to keep the bundles from moving around. Cover, bring gently to a boil and simmer for about 40 minutes, or until the rolls are tender and the rice is cooked. Add 1½ cups of water a few minutes before the end of cooking, as you will need it for the sauce.

Whisk the eggs, the juice of the remaining 3 lemons and a little salt and pepper in a bowl. Whisk in about a cup of the hot cooking liquid to acclimatize the egg, remove the pot from the heat, then pour the egg mixture into the pot. Distribute it by rocking the pot well. Return the pot to the lowest heat, shaking and rocking it until the sauce thickens a little. Be careful not to overheat it, as the eggs will scramble. If it doesn't look saucy enough, add a little hot water. Remove from the heat and let rest, covered, for a few minutes, rocking the pot now and then. Serve the rolls hot or warm, drizzled with a good amount of sauce, a light sprinkling of salt if necessary and a grinding of pepper.

KOKKINISTO REDDENED

Κοκκινιστό

SERVES 6

6 TABLESPOONS OLIVE OIL

6 9-OUNCE SLICES BEEF FOR STEWING (CHUCK OR BLADE) ABOUT 1¼ INCHES THICK

SALT

1 LARGE RED ONION, CHOPPED

½ CUP RED WINE

14-OUNCE CAN CRUSHED TOMATOES

1 TABLESPOON TOMATO PASTE

½ TEASPOON GROUND CINNAMON

2 TABLESPOONS CHOPPED ITALIAN PARSLEY

FRESHLY GROUND BLACK PEPPER

3 THYME SPRIGS

This is called reddened because, quite simply, the meat is cooked in a tomato sauce. Simple meat stews like this with tomato, and the lemonato on the opposite page, are very popular standard food in Greece. They would be served with some pasta on the side, or with french fries, which I love.

The fries in Greece often get an unusual sprinkling of cheese, which is wonderful and casual.

Preheat the oven to 350°F. Heat 3 tablespoons of olive oil in a large nonstick skillet and fry the beef until deep golden on both sides. Salt each side as it's done. Remove to a large cast-iron pot that has a lid. Add the rest of the olive oil and the onion to a pan and sauté until softened. Add the wine and cook until it has almost evaporated. Add the crushed tomatoes and the paste, the cinnamon and parsley, and season with a little salt and black pepper. Bring to a boil and simmer for a few minutes, smoothing out any big bits of tomato with a wooden spoon. Scrape over the beef. Fill the tomato can with water and add this to the pot. Add the thyme, cover with the lid and bake for about 2 hours, turning the meat a couple of times. Add an extra ½ cup of water, then bake for 30 minutes more. At the end of this time, the beef should be very tender and the sauce thick and jammy but abundant. If necessary, add a little hot water toward the end. Remove from the oven and serve.

LEMONATO LEMONED

Λεμονάτο

2 TABLESPOONS OLIVE OIL

3 TABLESPOONS BUTTER

2 POUNDS 2 OUNCES BONELESS VEAL SHOULDER, TIED UP WITH STRING TO HOLD ITS SHAPE WHILE COOKING

SALT AND FRESHLY GROUND BLACK PEPPER

1 GARLIC CLOVE, PEELED

½ SMALL ONION

JUICE OF 1 LARGE LEMON

You can use beef here and cook it in thick slices like the previous tomato version if you prefer. This is best for me with fries that can be dipped into the sauce too, but it's also wonderful with pasta.

Heat the oil and butter in a not-too-big cast-iron baking dish or a nonstick pot in which the meat will fit compactly. Brown the veal, sprinkling the done side with salt and pepper as you go. Add the garlic and onion, sauté for a moment to make lightly golden, then add 1 cup of water and put the lid on. Simmer over very low heat for about 2 hours, turning it over a few times and adding ½ cup of water and the lemon juice 15 minutes before the end. It should be soft, with a good amount of lemony sauce. Add a little extra water if needed. Remove the onion and garlic. Take off the heat and let rest in the pot, still covered, for 10 minutes before slicing and serving.

ΠΙΚΛΕΣ

ΒΑΡΟΣ ΚΑΘ. ΣΤΡΑΓΓΙΣΜΕΝΟ 5 ΚΙΛΑ

ΒΑΡΟΣ ΜΙΚΤΟ 9 ΚΙΛΑ

ΣΗΜΑ ΚΑΤΑΤΕΘΕΝ

TIS ORAS

THERE + THEN FOODS

How to order in Greece: once you have taken your table in a taverna—say on the beach—you could flip-flop your way inside to see the food. After choosing a few mezedes for the middle of the table to start with, as an entrée you could choose between the ready-cooked foods on display or the "there and then" foods, which are mostly grilled (or fried). These are often on display raw and include fish, meat skewers, and so on. You can usually just indicate by pointing to a dish and saying, "parakalo" (please).

PSARI LADOLEMONO GRILLED FISH WITH LEMON OIL

Ψάρι λαδολέμονο

SERVES 4

¼ CUP BEST-QUALITY OLIVE OIL

JUICE OF 1 LARGE JUICY LEMON

1 GARLIC CLOVE, PEELED

2 SEA BREAM (ABOUT 1 POUND 2 OUNCES EACH), SCALED AND CLEANED

SALT AND FRESHLY GROUND BLACK PEPPER

OLIVE OIL, FOR BRUSHING

ALATOPIPERIGANO (PAGE 128), FOR SERVING

2 TABLESPOONS COARSELY CHOPPED ITALIAN PARSLEY, FOR SERVING

This is the kind of thing to order on a Greek beach. It is extremely simple and good served with a dish of olives, some capers and some boiled vegetables dressed with olive oil on the side.

For grilling fish whole, it is good to have a double-sided grill rack so that you can just flip over the fish. This dish is also fantastic when done in the oven; salt and pepper the fish and roast it in a roasting dish with a couple of tablespoons of olive oil at 400°F. Half an hour for a fish of this size should do it. Then make the lemon oil, pour over the fish and serve.

Make the lemon oil by whipping the olive oil and lemon juice together in a small bowl until creamy. Add the whole garlic clove and put aside for the flavors to steep. Rinse the fish inside and out, and cut off their fins. Pat them dry with paper towels. Scatter their insides with salt, and salt and lightly pepper their outer skin.

Preheat a grill to hot. Position the rack about 4 inches from the coals and brush it with olive oil. Lay the fish on top and grill until the underside is golden and crusty here and there. Turn them over and grill the other side too. Transfer to a platter. Take the garlic clove out of the lemon oil and give it a final whip before drizzling over the fish. Scatter well with alatopiperigano, then a nice sprinkling of parsley. Serve hot, with an extra bowl for the bones.

BARBOUNIA TIGANITA FRIED RED MULLET

Μπαρμπούνια τηγανιτά

This simple dish of fried fish served with lemon is much loved in Greece. It would be ideal eaten while looking out at the sea, but in any setting it is very good. Nice served with a salad and horta.

Rinse the fish and pat dry with paper towels. Cut off the fins. Put the fish into a wide colander and splash well on both sides with the vinegar, then leave them for a few minutes. Put the flour in a large deep plate and stir through some salt and a few grinds of black pepper.

Fill a deep bowl with cold water. Dip each fish in the flour, coating both sides. Now quickly dip them in the cold water, shake, and coat them all over in flour once again.

Pour oil into a large skillet to a depth of ⅝ to ¾ inch and put over high heat. Fry the fish, turning them once, until crisp and golden on both sides. If they don't all fit, do them in batches. Remove to a plate lined with paper towels. Serve hot with a sprinkling of salt, the lemons and a plate for the bones.

MARIDA/ATHERINA TIGANITI FRIED TINY FISH

Μαρίδα/Αθερίνα τηγανιτή

SERVES 2

A COUPLE OF HANDFULS OF TINY FISH, SUCH AS WHITEBAIT OR SMELT

FLOUR, FOR COATING

SALT AND FRESHLY GROUND BLACK PEPPER

LIGHT OLIVE OIL, FOR FRYING

LEMON QUARTERS, FOR SERVING, OPTIONAL

These are fried until crisp and eaten whole, like french fries. You can use whitebait or any other tiny fish that can be eaten whole.

Rinse the fish and pat them dry with paper towels. Put some flour in a wide shallow bowl and season the flour with some salt and a few grinds of pepper.

Pour olive oil into a skillet to a depth of ¾ to 1¼ inches and put over high heat. Working in a couple of batches, toss the fish in the flour to coat, then fry them until crispy golden, turning them with a slotted spoon to ensure even frying. Remove to a plate lined with paper towels and sprinkle with a little salt as soon as they are all done. Serve with lemon for whoever wants.

KOLIOS (YOUNA) SUN-DRIED MACKEREL

Γούνα (κολιός)

SERVES 4

4 MACKEREL (ABOUT
10½ OUNCES EACH),
CLEANED

ABOUT 2 TEASPOONS SALT

FRESHLY GROUND BLACK
PEPPER

1 HEAPING TEASPOON
DRIED OREGANO

OLIVE OIL, FOR SERVING

LEMON QUARTERS,
FOR SERVING

My friend Kimon told me about this recipe first. I was intrigued, then found it on the island of Naxos with a potato salad that I have also given the recipe for (page 225). This fish is wonderful, unusual and very easy. It has a deep and honest flavor. It also goes well with something simple such as boiled zucchini and a lettuce and dill salad. Start with taramosalata, koulouria and maybe a dish of vinegared octopus.

Of course, this should only be done on a sunny day, and the amount of time the mackerel will need in the sun will depend on the strength of the sun. When salting fish, note that you need enough salt to dry as well as flavor it, but too much will ruin the flavor.

Cut the heads off the fish (or better, get your fishmonger to do it), slit through the belly and remove the innards. Gently open them, leaving the spine in place on one side with the tail. Pick out any bones from the spineless half, rinse and pat dry with paper towels. Sprinkle both sides generously with salt (roughly ¼ teaspoon on each side so each fish gets ½ teaspoon of salt) and a few grinds of pepper and lay the fish on a tray, skin side down. Crumble the oregano over and cover. Put out to dry in full sun for 5 to 6 hours, depending on the strength of the sun. Check now and then that they are drying but not shriveling up.

Preheat a grill to very hot. Brush the grill with a little oil and add the fish, skin side down, 3¼ to 4 inches from the coals. Grill until the skin is nice and crusty, then carefully turn the fish and grill just long enough for it to be gold here and there, but not dried out. Serve with a drizzle of olive oil and a good squeeze of lemon juice.

SOUVLAKI SE KALAMAKI PORK SKEWERS

Σουβλάκι (σε καλαμάκι)

MAKES ABOUT 12 SKEWERS

WOODEN SKEWERS (KALAMAKI)

2 POUNDS 10 OUNCES LEAN PORK WITH SOME FAT

2 TEASPOONS DRIED OREGANO

SALT AND FRESHLY GROUND BLACK PEPPER

3 TABLESPOONS OLIVE OIL

ABOUT 12 SLICES COUNTRY BREAD, ABOUT ¾ INCH THICK, HALVED IF LARGE

2 LEMONS, QUARTERED, FOR SERVING

These can either be wrapped in pita with tzatziki, tomatoes, lemon and parsley, as in the kebabs (page 288), or served as they are with some grilled bread. Here then, extra oregano and salt should be scattered on and lemon wedges served on the side.

Use a part of the pork toward the shoulder, where it's more tender. Pork fillets also work very well; just make sure you don't dry out the meat during grilling, as they have little fat.

Soak the skewers in cold water for about 30 minutes so they won't burn when they go over the coals. Trim any drastic fat off the pork, but leave some on for flavor and moistness. Cut the meat into rough ¾-inch cubes. Thread 6 pork cubes onto each skewer, leaving space at the top to spike the bread.

Put the skewers onto a plate, sprinkle with the oregano that you crush between your fingers, a little salt, and pepper. Drizzle the oil over and turn to coat evenly.

Preheat a grill to high and put the rack about 4 inches from the coals. Grill the souvlaki until nice and grilled looking here and there and still moist, not dry inside. Grill the bread lightly on both sides and spike it on the end of the skewers. Serve on a plate, or on squares of parchment paper, scattering over some extra salt and oregano. Serve hot, with lemon juice squeezed over.

KEBAB

Κεμπάπ

SERVES 4

9 OUNCES FINELY
GROUND LAMB

9 OUNCES FINELY
GROUND BEEF

1 SMALL RED ONION,
GRATED

2 TABLESPOONS COARSELY
CHOPPED ITALIAN PARSLEY

½ TEASPOON DRIED
OREGANO, CRUMBLED

SALT

11 THICK METAL SKEWERS

4¼ OUNCES TOMATOES
(ABOUT 3), QUARTERED

OLIVE OIL, FOR BRUSHING

FRESHLY GROUND BLACK
PEPPER

8 PITA BREADS, BOUGHT
OR HOMEMADE (PAGE 158)

1 SMALL RED ONION,
SLICED, FOR SERVING

A COUPLE OF HANDFULS
COARSELY CHOPPED
ITALIAN PARSLEY, FOR
SERVING

TZATZIKI (PAGE 130),
FOR SERVING

LEMON QUARTERS,
FOR SERVING

PAPRIKA IN A SHAKER,
FOR SERVING

8 SQUARES PARCHMENT
PAPER, ROUGHLY
10 INCHES

There are foods that are taken from neighboring countries and immigrants that then become a fixed item, such as kebabs, which have Turkish origins.

The ground meat here should have a little fat and the kebabs must be cooked over very hot coals so that they are nicely charred but still moist inside. If you don't have the skewers, you can just pat the meat into sausage shapes and grill anyway. Eating two of these in pita is not unreasonable if you are not having anything else.

The thing about eating these is that the warm juice runs the length of the meat into the pita, like a small stream in a current, and pools in the bottom, dripping inevitably through the soaked paper onto your hand. So you will need some heavy-duty wet wipes—or simply apologize to the next people you are introduced to or run into and have to kiss on both cheeks.

Put the lamb, beef, grated onion, parsley and oregano in a bowl and add ¾ to 1 teaspoon salt. Knead together thoroughly. Divide into 8 balls of about 2¾ ounces each. Firmly press each ball compactly around a skewer in a long sausage shape about 6 inches long. Thread 4 tomato quarters on each of the remaining skewers, making sure that you pierce through the skin so that they hold well.

Preheat a grill to high and brush it lightly with olive oil. Grill the meat kebabs until deep gold and slightly crusty in parts on the outside and still moist on the inside, but not dried out. Brush the tomatoes with a little olive oil, scatter lightly with salt and pepper and grill them at the same time. Brush the pita very lightly with olive oil on both sides (or leave plain if you prefer) and put on the grill to warm up.

To serve, remove the skewers from the kebabs. Halve the tomato quarters. Put a square of parchment paper on each plate and then 1 pita on top of each of these. Add a meat kebab, a couple of pieces of tomato, some onion slices, a good amount of parsley, a nice dab of tzatziki, a squeeze of lemon juice and a shaking of paprika. Add salt if you like. Roll up the pita quite tightly, then roll the paper around. Tuck the bottom in and leave the top third of the pita out. Eat. Move on to your second one. Then follow with a nice ice cream.

Greek (dried) oregano has a deep, intense and yet not overpowering flavor. I like to think that while these herbs are growing, they must somehow capture the mountains, sea, ambiance and Greek love in their growth, in their leaves. And then they are pulled from the earth, dried up in bundles in our homes, for all of the above to be unleashed into our pots and on our food when the oregano lands. So use Greek oregano if possible.

BIFTEKIA GRILLED BEEF BURGERS

Μπιφτέκια

MAKES 16

4 SLICES CRUSTLESS WHITE BREAD

2¼ POUNDS GROUND BEEF, WITH SOME FAT

1 EGG, LIGHTLY BEATEN

1 MEDIUM-LARGE RED ONION, GRATED ON THE LARGE HOLES OF A GRATER

3 HEAPING TABLESPOONS COARSELY CHOPPED ITALIAN PARSLEY

1 TABLESPOON CHOPPED MINT

1 RIPE TOMATO, GRATED ON THE LARGE HOLES OF A GRATER (SO THE SKIN STAYS BEHIND IN YOUR HAND)

SALT AND FRESHLY GROUND BLACK PEPPER

2 LEMONS, QUARTERED, FOR SERVING

These are definitely best grilled over charcoal, but you could also cook them in a griddle pan as a second option. They can be prepared beforehand and kept in the fridge; it's a great feeling to open the fridge and find it all done when you're in that last-minute rush of getting everything together at once. I like to serve these with simple things, like roast lemon potatoes, a tomato salad and bread.

Tear the bread into pieces and put in a bowl with about a cup of water. Soak for 10 minutes or so. Put the beef into a bowl and add the egg, onion, parsley, mint and tomato. Season well with salt and pepper. Squeeze out the excess water from the bread with your hands. If necessary press the bread in a fine-mesh sieve to make sure all the water is squeezed out. The mixture here is very soft, which is important for the end result, but the soaked bread must be very well squeezed out or the burgers won't hold their shape. Add the bread to the bowl. Mix it together, making sure everything is incorporated, then knead well to give a lovely soft mixture. Divide into 16 balls of about 3¼ ounces each. Shape into firm flat ovals about 4¼ × 2¾ inches and put on a tray. Keep in the fridge while you get your grill heated to very hot (or if you won't be cooking them immediately).

Brush the grill very lightly with oil, then cook the burgers on the grill about 4 inches away from the coals, pressing them gently with a metal spatula to keep their shape. When the undersides are deep golden, turn and do the other side. They should be crusty dark gold here and there but still moist inside. Sprinkle with a little salt and serve at once, with lemon quarters.

SWEET FOODS

As close up and alive and now as the Greeks may be, there is an incredible feeling of past and tradition embroidered through their linens and laces. And a knowing that you could just turn up at someone's house for the first time and enter through the back door. It is a nation not styled and sitting pretty. Not one of those distant, unreachable races. But a lot of loud, late-celebrating nights and sleeping-in, coffee-drinking, communicating tavli players who love their history and their country. Of uncles pinching your cheeks till they hurt. And aunts' large arms waiting to embrace you. Of desserts drenched with Greek love and syrup.

You may as well surrender.

KARPOUZI ME FETA WATERMELON + FETA

Καρπούζι με φέτα

1 WATERMELON

FETA

Not quite a dessert, more a Greek snack. On a hot summer's day to sit under a Greek tree at the end of a road or on a beach and see miles of endless sea, with watermelon, feta and a knife must be one of the greatest things in realizing the spacings that exist in Greece. This is wonderful, sweet and salty. Great.

Cut off the rind, then slice the watermelon flesh into chunks and put on a plate. Break the feta into chunks and eat with the watermelon. That's it.

IPOVRIHIO SUBMARINE

Υποβρύχιο

MAKES ABOUT 2 CUPS

3 CUPS PLUS 3 TABLESPOONS SUPERFINE SUGAR

1 VANILLA BEAN, SPLIT

1 TEASPOON LEMON JUICE

Old Greece. Love this. Greek children adore it. Very very sweet. Can be flavored with vanilla, rose, pistachio, lemon, and probably other flavors as well. It's so sugary and thick that you scoop it up and it clings to the spoon. You submarine that into a glass of ice-cold water, then lick the water off the spoon and some of the ipovrihio comes off as well. And on you go until it's all finished. Some people even like to drink the water then. One spoonful of this would seem enough, but then, sometimes they come and ask for more.

You can buy it anywhere in Greece. Or you could try this at home.

Put the sugar in a saucepan with 7 tablespoons of water. Stir until the sugar dissolves, add the vanilla bean, then bring to a boil. Simmer until thickened (when a blob of syrup dropped in a glass of cold water forms a soft ball, 234–241°F on a candy thermometer). Add the lemon juice and continue to boil for a minute or two, then remove from the heat.

Strain it into a bowl and leave to cool to lukewarm. It will turn white as it cools. Stir with a wooden spoon in the same direction until it thickens. To serve, scoop a spoonful and dip it into a glass of ice-cold water. Keeps well in an airtight container.

* *For rose ipovrihio, omit the vanilla bean and add (in the same direction) 2 teaspoons of rose water and a few drops of red food coloring just before you start stirring.*

YIAOURTI ME MELI
GREEK YOGURT,
HONEY + NUTS

Γιαούρτι με μέλι

SERVES 1

2 DOLLOPS OF
GREEK YOGURT

1 HEAPED TABLESPOON
BROKEN-UP SHELLED
WALNUT HALVES

GROUND CINNAMON,
FOR SCATTERING

ABOUT 2 TEASPOONS
THICK BUT DROP-OFF-
THE-SPOON HONEY

A fresh fruit cut up over this is also lovely. The nuts are nice lightly toasted in a dry skillet, but you may be having this on an island somewhere and not have your skillet with you. This is a lovely breakfast.

Dollop yogurt into a bowl. Sprinkle with walnuts, scatter on a little cinnamon, drizzle over some honey and give a final scattering of cinnamon.

GLIKO TOU KOUTALIOU SPOON SWEETS

Γλυκό του κουταλιού

EACH SERVES 9 TO 12

**CHERRY SPOON
SWEETS**

2½ CUPS SUGAR

1 POUND 2 OUNCES
LARGE SOUR OR UNDER-
RIPE CHERRIES

1 STRIP LEMON ZEST

1 TABLESPOON ALMOND
OR CHERRY LIQUEUR

———————

**CHESTNUT SPOON
SWEETS**

1 POUND 2 OUNCES FRESH
CHESTNUTS, SHELL ON

2½ CUPS SUGAR

1 TABLESPOON HONEY

1 TABLESPOON
LEMON JUICE

———————

There are many varieties of this very typical sweet: sour cherry, lemon blossom, rose petal, green walnut, chestnut, watermelon rind, fig, quince, baby clementine, apricot, grapes. . . . They are really lovely looking, lying in a thick syrup bath. You may be offered one when you visit someone, always with a glass of ice-cold water. The fruit pieces should not be too big, just large enough to fit on a small spoon, which you would dip (only once, of course) into the jar. Serve another spoon if people want more, but normally just one gives you enough of the sweetness you need.

For the cherry spoon sweets,
put the sugar in a large pan with 1 cup of water and stir until the sugar dissolves. Wash the cherries well and remove the stems. Pit them, then stir into the sugar and water. Leave to steep for 3 hours.

Add the lemon zest and liqueur. Without stirring, bring to a boil over high heat. Simmer for 5 to 6 minutes, skimming the surface with a slotted spoon as necessary. Remove the cherries with a slotted spoon and place in a sterilized preserving jar and continue cooking the syrup until it is very thick–230°F on a candy thermometer if you have one. Cool a little before pouring over the cherries and sealing.

For the chestnut spoon sweets,
prepare the chestnuts by cutting a cross in the shell of each one with a small sharp knife, being careful not to cut into the flesh. Bring a large pot of water to a boil and add half the chestnuts. Simmer for 5 minutes, then scoop out with a slotted spoon. Cool for a minute or two, then gently peel off the

shell. Repeat with the remaining chestnuts. Now put them all in a pot, cover with cold water and bring to a boil. Simmer until their skins loosen, just a few minutes, then drain. While still hot, gently rub them in a dish cloth to remove the skin still attached to the nut.

Put the sugar, honey and lemon juice in a pan with 1 cup of water and stir over medium heat until sugar dissolves. Add the chestnuts and bring to a boil. Simmer for 7 to 8 minutes. Remove the chestnuts with a slotted spoon and place in a sterilized preserving jar and continue cooking the syrup until it thickens, 230°F on a candy thermometer. Cool a little before pouring over the chestnuts and sealing.

For the quince spoon sweets,

peel, quarter and core the quinces. Cut the quarters into thick slices, large enough to fit on a dessert spoon. Put in a pot with 8 cups of water and bring to a boil. Simmer, covered, until the quinces turn a lovely gold-red, 2 to 3 hours depending on how ripe your quinces are. Check the water level from time to time and add more if necessary.

Put the sugar and 1 cup of the quince water in another pot and stir until the sugar dissolves. Using a slotted spoon, transfer the quince slices to the new pot and add the vanilla, cinnamon and lemon juice. Bring to a boil and simmer for 8 to 10 minutes. Remove the quinces with a slotted spoon and place in a sterilized preserving jar. Continue cooking the syrup until it thickens, 230°F on a candy

QUINCE SPOON SWEETS

3 QUINCES
2½ CUPS SUGAR
1 VANILLA BEAN, SPLIT
1 CINNAMON STICK
2 TEASPOONS LEMON JUICE

FIG SPOON SWEETS

2½ CUPS SUGAR
1 TABLESPOON HONEY
1 POUND 2 OUNCES FIRM UNDERRIPE FIGS
1 CINNAMON STICK
1 SMALL STRIP LEMON ZEST

**ME PIRE
O
IPNOS—
SLEEP
TOOK ME
(AND
CARRIED
ME FAR
AWAY . . .)**

continued

thermometer if you have one. Cool a little before pouring over the quinces and sealing.

For the fig spoon sweets,

put the sugar and honey in a large pan with 1 cup of water and stir until the sugar dissolves. Add the figs, cinnamon and lemon zest. Without stirring, bring to a boil, then simmer for about 8 minutes. Remove the figs gently with a slotted spoon and place them in a shallow bowl in a single layer. Continue cooking the syrup until it thickens, 230°F on a candy thermometer if you have one. Cool a little before pouring over the figs. Cool completely before putting in a sterilized preserving jar and sealing.

To sterilize the jars, lay a thick layer of newspaper or dish cloths on one or 2 oven racks (being careful to avoid the flame if using a gas oven) and preheat the oven to 350°F. Arrange the cleaned jars, opened end up, and their lids on the racks. Close the oven door and heat for 18 to 20 minutes. Using thick pot holders, remove each jar from the oven as needed and place on a thick layer of newspaper to fill. Avoid putting a hot jar on a cold surface. The oven temperature can be dropped to 300°F to hold the jars until you are ready to fill each one with hot food. If you are putting cold food in, it must go into cold jars.

KRASSOKOULOURA WINE RINGS

Κρασοκούλουρα

MAKES ABOUT 20

2 CUPS ALL-PURPOSE FLOUR

1 TEASPOON BAKING POWDER

½ CUP SUGAR

1 TEASPOON GROUND CINNAMON

¼ TEASPOON GROUND CLOVES

SALT

6 TABLESPOOONS OLIVE OIL

½ CUP WHITE WINE

Greece is full of koulouria and koulourakia (this is the much-used diminutive in Greek). Sweet and savory, there are many different varieties of these round cookies. Vanilla, citrus, sesame, cinnamon are some others you may come across. These are made with wine. They will last for quite a while in a cookie tin.

Preheat the oven to 350°F. Put the flour, baking powder, sugar, cinnamon and cloves in a bowl and add a pinch of salt. Stir with a wooden spoon to combine, then stir in the olive oil and wine. Mix with your hands, adding a little more flour or wine as necessary to get a soft, uniform dough. Knead well for a couple of minutes.

Divide the dough into oval balls of roughly 1 ounces each. Let rest at room temperature, uncovered, for about 5 minutes. Using your hands, roll each out into a rope 10 inches or so long. Join the ends and pat one end over the other to close the bracelet. Put as many as will fit onto a baking sheet lined with parchment paper and bake for 20 to 25 minutes, or until crisp and golden. Bake the rest.

LOUKOUMI ROSE DELIGHT

Λουκούμι

MAKES 28 PIECES

2 CUPS SUGAR

1 TEASPOON LEMON JUICE

½ CUP CORNSTARCH

½ TEASPOON CREAM OF TARTAR

2 TEASPOONS ROSE WATER

3 TABLESPOONS SHELLED PISTACHIOS, HALVED LENGTHWISE

RED FOOD COLORING

¼ CUP CONFECTIONERS' SUGAR, FOR COATING

2 TABLESPOONS CORNSTARCH, EXTRA FOR COATING

These are most well known as Turkish delight. They are the sweets you are offered when you stop in at someone's place, even just for a quick visit. They are served with a glass of cold water. Loukoumia are also beautiful cut up into very small squares and served next to a coffee. The island of Syros is well known for their loukoumi. They are often flavored with rose, masticha or pistachio.

A sugar thermometer is important here to tell you when the sugar syrup is at the right stage.

Put the sugar and lemon juice in a pan with ¾ cup of water. Stir until the sugar dissolves. Bring to a boil. Simmer without stirring for 30 or 40 minutes, or until a small dab is soft and pliable between your fingers when it's dropped into cold water (soft ball stage or 240°F on a candy thermometer).

Combine the cornstarch and cream of tartar in a heavy-bottomed saucepan and whisk in 1½ cups water until smooth. Cook on medium heat, stirring constantly, until thick. Slowly stir in the sugar syrup. Simmer over very low heat until very thick and pale golden, 60 to 70 minutes. Stir often to ensure that your mixture isn't sticking to the pan. Brush an 8¼ × 4½-inch dish with straight sides with oil and line with plastic wrap. Stir the rose water and pistachios into the mixture and add the coloring drop by drop until you have a soft rose-petal pink. Pour into the dish and cool overnight, covered.

Combine the confectioners' sugar and cornstarch on a plate. Cut the loukoumi into 1¼-inch squares and toss in the sugar mix. It will keep for weeks in a covered tin or box, not an airtight container.

YIAOURTOPITA YOGURT CAKE

Γιαουρτόπιτα

MAKES 1 CAKE

¾ CUP PLUS 1 TABLESPOON (13 TABLESPOONS) BUTTER, ROOM TEMPERATURE

1⅓ CUPS SUGAR

3 EGGS

1 TEASPOON VANILLA EXTRACT

2 CUPS ALL-PURPOSE FLOUR

1 TABLESPOON BAKING POWDER

SALT

1 CUP GREEK YOGURT

I love this for its damp crumbs and great texture. It's the kind of cake that can be taken just about anywhere and it will be the right thing.

Preheat the oven to 350°F and butter and flour a 9½-inch spring-form pan. Beat the butter and sugar together with handheld beaters until pale. Add the eggs one at a time, beating well after each addition. Add the vanilla and beat in well. Add the flour, baking powder and a pinch of salt together with the yogurt, and beat until thick and smooth. Spoon into the pan.

Bake for about 45 minutes, or until a skewer inserted into the center comes out clean. The cake should be lovely and moist, so be careful not to overbake it. Check after about 30 minutes and cover the surface with foil if it is browning too quickly. Remove from the oven and cool in the pan for 10 to 15 minutes before turning out onto a wire cake rack.

MOUSTALEVRIA GRAPE JUICE PUDDING

Μουσταλευριά

MAKES ABOUT 15 SQUARES

2¾ POUNDS SEEDLESS RED GRAPES

1 TABLESPOON SUGAR

½ TEASPOON GROUND CINNAMON

3 TABLESPOONS PLUS 2 TEASPOONS CORNSTARCH

1 TABLESPOON SESAME SEEDS

You can make this from red or green grapes—muscats would be lovely. But the type of grapes you use are very important for the color as well as the flavor. Here I have used Concord grapes, which give an amazing intensity of color and taste.

The best way to extract the juice is to put them through a juicer, and bear in mind that you may need more or fewer grapes, depending on how much juice they have.

This can also be served in small bowls as a pudding, in which case use a little less cornstarch. Moustalevria is traditionally a worker's food, given to those who help with the harvest, so it is most often eaten in September.

Blend the grapes in a blender or food processor until liquid and sieve out the skins, or pass them through a juicer. If you can't get seedless grapes, you will have to use a juicer. You will need 3 cups of juice, so you can drink any left over. Put the juice into a pot, bring to a boil and simmer uncovered for about 15 minutes, skimming the surface of scum with a slotted spoon. Add the sugar and cinnamon halfway through. Put the cornstarch into a cup and stir in 3 tablespoons of cold water, mixing it until smooth. Gradually stir this into the simmering grape juice. Whisk over low heat until it has thickened a lot to a creamy pudding, about 15 minutes. Scrape into a rectangular dish of roughly 7 × 5 inches and level the surface. Cool a little before scattering with the sesame seeds. Cool completely and refrigerate overnight before cutting into squares.

PAGOTO KAIMAKI SALEPI + MASTICHA ICE CREAM

Παγωτό καϊμάκι

SERVES 6 TO 8

½ TEASPOON MASTICHA GRANULES

¾ CUP PLUS 1½ TABLESPOONS SUGAR

3 CUPS MILK

2 TEASPOONS GROUND SALEPI (ORCHID ROOT)

¾ CUP LIGHT CREAM

This has a very definite, almost chewy texture that is instantly recognizable.

I went to a spice shop in the heart of Athens to buy the salepi (orchid root) needed, and the man spun around when I mentioned it; he was clearly happy that I would be making kaimaki and started thus to recite his recipe. He mimed and mimicked and gesticulated, rambling along his Greek road of youth. He explained, plucking his finger out of the imaginary hot milk, that we would now be ready to stir in the rest. Then came the stirring motion of the wooden spoon and the handheld beaters next, which were so realistically beating against the sides of the bowl with his clucking that I almost imagined that the ice cream would be appearing out of thin air any moment.

Grind the masticha with a little of the sugar to make dust. This is best done in a spice grinder, but a mortar and pestle is fine too. Put the rest of the sugar in a pot with the milk and heat to just below the boiling point. Take off the heat and whisk in the ground masticha and salepi, and keep whisking until they are all dissolved. Leave to cool. Whisk in the cream, then pour into an ice-cream machine and freeze according to the manufacturer's instructions. Alternatively, pour into a shallow baking sheet and put in the freezer. When it starts to set, beat it well with a fork to break up the ice crystals. Repeat this 3 or 4 more times until the ice cream is smooth and solid.

OUZO SORBET

Σορμπέ ούζου

SERVES 6 TO 8

1 CUP SUGAR
7 TABLESPOONS OUZO

This is like a soft snow, sweet and ouzo-y, and it works well after a meal— like an after-dinner mint.

Stir the sugar into 3 cups of water and bring to a boil. Simmer for 5 minutes. Cool. Stir in the ouzo and transfer to an ice-cream machine. Freeze following the manufacturer's instructions. Alternatively, pour into a shallow baking sheet and put in the freezer, breaking it up and beating with a fork 3 or 4 times before it becomes solid.

KEIK PORTOKALI ORANGE SEMOLINA CAKE

Κέικ σιμιγδαλένιο με πορτοκάλι

MAKES ABOUT 24 DIAMONDS

2 ORGANIC ORANGES (SUCH AS NAVEL), WELL SCRUBBED

SYRUP

⅔ CUP SUGAR

JUICE OF ¼ LEMON

1 TEASPOON ANTHONERO (FLOWER WATER SUCH AS LEMON OR ORANGE BLOSSOM)

¾ CUP OLIVE OIL

⅔ CUP SUGAR

5 EGGS

2 CUPS FINE SEMOLINA

4 TEASPOONS BAKING POWDER

½ CUP ALMONDS, CHOPPED

I got this recipe from my friend Artemis, who in turn got it from her friend Galatia. They serve it with Greek coffee. Sometimes with a scoop of ice cream on the side.

I have halved the syrup amount, but you decide after the first time whether you want to up the syrup again and make it more traditional, damper and sweeter.

Boil the whole oranges in plenty of water until softened, about 1 hour. Keep checking that they are well covered and add hot water as needed.

Preheat the oven to 350°F. Oil and flour a 9½-inch cake pan (not springform). Put the syrup ingredients in a saucepan with ¾ cup of water and stir over medium-high heat until the sugar dissolves. Bring to a boil and simmer uncovered for 6 to 7 minutes. Set aside to cool.

Quarter the oranges to check that there are no seeds. Puree them, skin and all, in a blender or food processor until you have a smooth orange mush. Pour this into a bowl and stir in the oil, sugar and eggs. Whip with beaters, then beat in the semolina, baking powder and almonds. Scrape out into the cake pan and bake until a skewer inserted in the center comes out clean, about 40 minutes. Cool the cake in the pan for 10 minutes or so. Still in the pan, cut it into diamonds about 2¾ inches long and 1½ inches across the middle. Gently pour the cooled syrup over the top, covering all the cake. Leave to cool completely before serving.

PASTELLI SESAME AND PISTACHIO SNACK

Παστέλι

MAKES ABOUT 30 SQUARES

¾ CUP PLUS 2 TEASPOONS SESAME SEEDS

⅓ CUP SHELLED PISTACHIOS, BROKEN IN HALF

¼ CUP SUGAR

¼ CUP MILD RUNNY HONEY

A very good, nutritious, sweet snack. Kids love to eat this at a paniyiri (a local fair honoring saints). In the good old days it was seen as a good thing, an extravagance—"finish your food and you can have a piece of pastelli." I love it with the pistachio nuts that the island of Aegina is so well known for.

It is very easy to make yourself, and the amount can easily be doubled. Keeps in an airtight container for many days.

Put the sesame seeds and pistachios into a nonstick skillet and toast lightly over low heat to color them. Add the sugar to the skillet and cook, without stirring, over low heat until it melts and becomes lightly golden. Standing back, add the honey. Stir in the sesame seeds and pistachios and mix while you can, as it will be sticky and thick.

Scrape out onto a flat, heatproof surface such as marble or a plastic pastry sheet, or even a large flat plate. Flatten it a bit with the back of a spoon, then use your hands dipped in cold water to form a rectangular shape. Use a rolling pin to level the surface and to stretch the rectangle to roughly 6 × 7 inches and ¼ inch thick. Wait for a few minutes, then cut into 1¼-inch squares (or rectangles). If you leave it standing for too long, it will become too hard to cut.

MELOPITA
HONEY CAKE

Μελόπιτα

SERVES 8

2 EGGS

3½ TABLESPOONS SUGAR

2 TABLESPOONS
ALL-PURPOSE FLOUR

4½ TABLESPOONS HONEY

1 TABLESPOON LEMON
JUICE

1 TABLESPOON BRANDY

1 POUND 2 OUNCES
SOFT MIZITHRA CHEESE OR
RICOTTA

1 TABLESPOON SUGAR,
EXTRA

1 HEAPING TEASPOON
GROUND CINNAMON

You will need a round ceramic dish of about 10 inches. I love this served with figs, either fresh or roasted with a little honey and sesame seeds. I have added a splash of brandy to the simple but lovely ingredients here.

Preheat the oven to 350°F. Butter and flour a 10-inch ovenproof round ceramic dish. Put the eggs and sugar into a bowl and beat using handheld beaters until voluminous, creamy and thick. Beat in the flour. Add the honey, lemon juice and brandy, and tip in the mizithra. Whisk well until it's thick, creamy and ribbony. Scrape into the baking dish and rock it to distribute evenly. Bake until a bit golden, about 30 minutes. Scatter the extra sugar and sieve the cinnamon over the top. Serve at room temperature or cover and refrigerate, as it is also good cold.

KAFES ELLINIKOS GREEK COFFEE

Ελληνικός Καφές

The muddy-on-the-bottom, thick and great-tasting coffee served in small cups is the kind you'll find the older generation in particular drinking. You need a small coffee pot (briki), which is available in different sizes. When ordering, you will be asked how you want your coffee: glyki (sweet), metrio (medium) or sketo (no sugar). The sugar is stirred into the water with the ground coffee before heating. Before drinking, it needs to sit for a minute so the sediment can fall to the bottom of the cup.

When you have finished your coffee, maybe you can find a Greek woman who knows about these things to read your cup for you. Or turn it upside down and let the coffee remains dribble down into the shapes that they will take. And then you can interpret interesting stories. A long line surely means a journey?

Fill your Greek coffee cup with room temperature water to more or less the level you want your coffee. Tip that into the briki and add 1 heaped teaspoonful of Greek coffee. Stir in 2 teaspoons of sugar for sweet (glyki), 1 teaspoon for medium (metrio), and no sugar for sketo. Put the briki over medium-high heat and remove from the heat just before it reaches a rolling boil. Cool momentarily before repeating, not allowing it to boil, as this can destroy the froth (kaimaki). (If your froth has bubbles in it, they say it must mean love—one way or another . . .)

Serve with a glass of cold water.

INDEX

Acknowledgments

A big and humble thank-you to all who helped me put this book together.

To my team: photographer Manos, stylist Michail and art director Lisa—thank you from the bottom of my heart. I would never have made it to page 2 without you. A very big thank-you to Jo and Luisa for all your wonderful and much-needed help.

Thank you, Lisa M.G, for all your support and encouragement always, and to all my friends at home for helping me in your various ways: thanks Anjalika, Mariella, Joan, Andrea, Rebecca, Peta, Anabelle, Scilla, Roberto, Leontine, Patrizia, Tanya, Balthazar, Didi, Corinne, Marion, Theo, Luciano and Stefania.

From my Greek side of things, thank you all for your big contributions, I am always grateful: thank you to my Greek angel helpers Anais, Danille and Katerina and to Artemis, Kyriakos, Christina, Galatia, Emily, Niko P, Roulla . . . thank you to Ketty, Nikola, Uncle Makis, Niko T, Anette, Kiki, Iria, Irini, Katerina, Kimon, Maria, Ariana, Minnie, Mr. Angelos, Kiria Fotini, Virginia, Angela, Elpida, Leta, Elsa and Maria.

To my publisher, Kay, thank you for possibility. And to all at Murdoch—especially Daniela and Vivien—thank you for your support and everything that you have given the book.

To Mom, Dad, Nin and Ludi: thank you, thank you, and to Santo Giovanni and Cassia and Yasmine— thank you for all that you are.

Tess xx